WAKING UP IN ASIA

WAKING UP IN ASIA

KIM M. HOOD

EDITED BY
DENISE M. WALKER

Armor of Hope Writing and Publishing Services, LLC.

Copyright © 2020 Kim M. Hood

ISBN: 978-1-64718-267-0

All rights reserved. No part of this publication may be reproduced, stored in a retrieval system, or transmitted in any form or by any means, electronic, mechanical, recording or otherwise, without the prior written permission of the author.

Armor of Hope Writing and Publishing Services, LLC.

Printed on acid-free paper.

Armor of Hope Writing and Publishing Services, LLC.
2020

First Edition

Cover and Interior Design by: Gracena Gray, Gathering House Publishing

Editing by: Denise M. Walker, Armor of Hope Writing and Publishing Services, LLC

DEDICATION

Dedicated to the memory of the
April 27, 2011 Tornado Victims

TABLE OF CONTENTS

Intro 1

Nightmares from Lard Yao 5

The King's Court 10

Hospital Reject Tea 33

Nefarious Nigerian Neighbors 41

Daymares 48

Monsoon Years 60

Fed-Con Air Express 74

Seven Calendars 166

Outro 196

INTRO

It took four Thai police officers and two DEA agents, to escort me through the airport. We were rushing to the prisoner transport van. I didn't understand why though. Captured and vulnerable, there was no escaping. My handcuffs were tight. They were moving me along the Don Mueang International fast. It was as if we were range walking. I figuratively had tainted blood on my hands already, from a pending domestic violence case. Now, I was seeing red out of anger and embarrassment. I didn't know what the hell I was doing. Being arrested in Bangkok, while out of jail on a bond in Alabama, would be unexplainable to my parents. They were under the impression I was doing quite well in Birmingham. I wasn't supposed to be out of my home state, let alone the country. Recklessly, I'd attempted to carry several kilos of heroin onto an aircraft, bound for The United States of America. After the DEA agents had taken photos of the drug seizure, video footage was recorded. Afterwards, I was hurriedly marched out of the building, and loaded into a vehicle. I was informed of my destination and quickly whisked away. With each bump on the uneven highway, my thoughts were going off kilter. So unimaginable it all was! I'd gone from never having any legal troubles in my life to now being charged with two major felonies within the same year. It was a sickening state of affairs. I couldn't do anything, but think about one question repeatedly, while on the drive to the local Thai jail for in-processing. Why did I get out of the military and start gravitating towards desperate people? Willingly, I'd opened my arms and taken their bait. For the wellbeing and safety's sake of two children, I'd made some dangerous decisions from the start.

Being a disabled veteran and ex-postal service worker, I know the held importance of individual freedoms. Events that are shared within the following pages have since come and gone. The relevance to current times, and difficult situations some people still fall prey to, will never cease. I'd managed to accomplish a lot of my goals before, during, and after getting out of the military in late December 1991.

Unforeseen circumstances temporarily dashed the hopes and dreams of my future in 1994. That's the year I landed inside of an Asian prison. The vehicle that was used in my public downfall is being turned around. It's an opportunity to have some healthy dialogue. About the routes we all take, whether good or bad, throughout our trajectory of life.

I'd never had a problem with making friends or elocution. However, talking too much behind prison walls can be misinterpreted with detrimental results.

The information was disseminated from The United States Embassy, during the incoming briefing. Ensuring the stakes were clearly understood by all newcomers, they would come out to see the American women and men, at least once a month for official visits. Checking on our safety during incarceration and conducting various monetary transactions was a part of their busy schedules. They also relayed any family emergency information, which couldn't wait for the mail system.

"What on earth made you think it was a good idea to jeopardize your bond and travel off to another country?" That was one of the most asked questions I'd received from several of the missionaries. They'd heard rumors about my cases from the newspapers.

Genuine interest in the details of what happened to me was appreciated. My position was oblique and evasive for fear of judgment. The missionaries, who came inside of the compound visitation area, were there to take care of the shopping needs for the non-local prisoners. I was on their list as one of the inmates, who had money on their account books. It was an ongoing insider joke amongst the few dozen American women. The more Thai baht we had would definitely keep the visits coming in regularly.

I'd decided shortly after sentencing, one of my frequent visitors, who was a German man, would be the person with whom I would open up to about my many sagas. He'd recently left a well-paying job to travel the globe. His latest stop was in Thailand, only a few months before I'd arrived. Listening to the reasons he'd given behind leaving his long-standing job and becoming a missionary were some of the most intriguing one's I'd ever heard. I didn't know how many chances we'd get to see each other. Only twenty-minute durations set when we did have visitation would be a hindrance. I was willing to tell him the unadulterated truth slowly, every week if given an opportunity.

I wouldn't say to him I'd been duped into despicable acts. That was the perception many had gathered from the bits and pieces they'd heard about me. The heavy yolk of silence needed to be lifted from my shoulders. A small breakthrough was coming, after a couple years of silent confinement. I was ready to burst. I'd built a well-crafted moving fortress revolving around the premise, "Nothing this bad could ever happen in my world." Unfortunately, for me the precision hadn't been correct with that calculation.

There was no communication with family members, other than through the mail or the U. S. Embassy. It was a harsh penalty to endure. When speaking with one particular missionary, like a lifeline phone system during my imprisonment, made me realize at lot of things. If I dealt with what issues I'd wanted to avoid the most, it could be an invaluable lesson until freedom came back to me.

NIGHTMARES FROM LARD YAO

It was nicknamed The Notorious Bangkok Hilton long before my arrival inside. The official name is Lard Yao Women's Remand Home. Its location is centered deep within the walls of Klong Prem Central Prison in Bangkok, Thailand. In my late twenties, I spent four and a half years out of my life as an inmate, inside of the one-hundred-year-old Draconian compound.

It took me two years after being incarcerated, before I'd felt any real considerations about opening up to talk. I was ready to speak to someone about the actual facts, surrounding my involvement with international drug trafficking smugglers from Nigeria. At the time of my arrest, I was out on bond for another serious charge. Though sketchy, the allegation stemming from one of the crimes was true, but complicated. Technically speaking, I did attempt to board an aircraft, heading into The United States of America with over six kilos of heroin. However, that wasn't a part of my original plans.

During my years of being confined in the mid 1990's, I was a witness to unbearable horrors. My intent was to steer clear in order to survive them. The warden arbitrarily walked through the main section of the compound. She wasn't intrusive to the inmates. The guards were to be addressed as Khun's, and a few of them were corrupt agitators. Several times it was confirmed in the press from findings made public by Amnesty International. They were constantly investigating reports of isolated abuses.

The conditions were inhumane with close to one-thousand women packed in like pickles. They had us housed similar to cattle and sleeping on the floor. Several of the ladies were drug addicts, enduring different stages of withdrawal. They were some of the sickest individuals I'd ever encountered. Tuberculosis, skin diseases, conjunctivitis, psychological issues, and a host of other maladies befell several Thai inmates. I wanted no parts of their germs or problems.

The cells were ancient with old teak hardwood floors, except for the newest building. Most Americans were clamoring to move into it. It had cork board flooring and a modern concept. The free food was prepared unsafely, but the majority of the compound had to eat it. The sound from animals scurrying around at night was noticeably creepy.

No glass windows, only screens and steel bars. Four multi-level buildings were used as sleeping quarters. Three guard shacks, two cheap labor workstations, and several other non-descript buildings were used for miscellaneous purposes. There was a building for the laundry, a chow hall, bakery, a hospital, arts & crafts room, salon, nursery, and the outside visitation area.

There was no bottled water. A huge onsite tank was used. It had a continuous heavy running stream of water, flowing from its reservoir. We had to catch several jugs each day. Inexpensive prison commissary food in a bag was available. They called it a Lanka store, where we purchased it all. If we had money on our prison account, it was ours to shop in at least twice a day. If we couldn't afford our own food, rice and fried duck eggs, or watery ratatouille was served to us.

A small tree house was used for segregation. It was an 8' x 6' punishment box for the disobedient. It was a visually frightening intimidator. They oftentimes left those girls baking in the steaming heat for days before allowing them to come down. Their buddies would consistently risk a similar fate of joining them. The Thai inmates would throw their buddies small baggies of water, ice, or food. Someone else would distract the guard, who watched occasionally from a slight vantage point. They tried one time to put an American up there for fighting, but the warden denied the request immediately. I had associates from other countries who'd endured its torture. They were changed for the worst.

Like most third world countries in the early 1990's, the showers were outside. Several open outhouses were spread throughout the four corners of the yard. It was absolutely mortifying having a bowel movement. There were women walking past us and glancing while we attempted to do the business.

Being incarcerated is a boring waste of time. The unique setting of neatly trimmed grass and opulent gardens scattered throughout the grounds. The guards had certain Thai inmate's landscape, giving off an efflorescence effect. They were mainly smoke screens, planted to keep us away from the underlying maelstrom of our emotions.

Every day felt doubly worse. Knowing the confines of Lard Yao was halfway across the globe. It was an ocean away from my family. In a godforsaken country that faithfully worshipped a king daily like he was their father.

Yesterday is the same as tomorrow, and tomorrow will be no different than the previous day. Next month will mirror last month, but it can only be as monotonous and wasted to the extent we allowed it to be. I'd tried to immerse myself with reading, writing letters to family, friends, and taking several long walks around the compound daily. The most dangerous kind of woman is one filled with apprehensiveness. Crammed and supplanted inside of a tiny area and surrounded by hundreds of hormonal females who're all in the same inescapable, humidity filled hot box. We had to figure out the best way to get ourselves through it.

Being left to our own devices if we refused to work was accepted. If we weren't native to Thailand, the no forced labor rule was the only respite. No surveillance cameras to monitor inmates made finding hiding spots extremely easy. There were huge trees, and lockers outside of the buildings everywhere. We could also hang out periodically in the chow hall, or in the exercise area when the scorching heat became unbearable. The only real accountability given was at evening lockdown.

For the longest time, I'd flown under the radar. Eventually, there was a guy who I had allowed to be my confidant. He was a kind missionary named William from Germany. He frequently went out of his way to visit. After a couple of years, he'd convinced me to grant his wish of more elaborate conversations.

He was interested in what it takes to make it through the lonely days, and even longer nights spent living inside of a foreign prison. Discussions were also going to be about my military background. I'd agreed to speak freely with him. His constant questions would be answered on his next few visits, which was a huge step for me. There was a genuine feeling of looking forward to it. I finally wanted to talk about the archaic, concrete jungle where myself, and countless others found ourselves residing.

THE KING'S COURT

The clanking sound of keys unlocking the cell door, stirred away my morning thoughts. I refrained from making any movements. Usually I was awake before the guards came to let us out. With so many floors and buildings, it took them a while. It gave me time to reflect on the events from the previous evening and gather myself for the new day. Living inside of a confinement that's primitive with greenery everywhere, is akin to a picture of an uninhabited island, with lush valleys on a postcard. It may look interesting, but you don't want to live there! Having to survive outside twelve hours each day, rain or shine, is torturous. It was the daily routine inside of Lard Yao.

Being an avid nature lover, I was semi-built for the outdoors terrain. Having spent several years in the United States Army after high school, I'd embraced being out in the field a few days out of a year. That, however, was extreme on every level. We had to fend for ourselves and stay out of any type of trouble until lockdown, which was before dusk if we didn't work. I chose not to labor for them.

Care packages were coming in sporadically from the families who could afford to do so. A stipend of money was signed for and received every thirty days from the United States Embassy. All of the Americans were required to pay it back eventually. The consequence of failing to do so would be to never regain our passport.

Most of the inmates worked extremely hard in the factories, especially in the blue jeans, bakery, and arts sections. Several Thai's sold small quantities of some type of tobacco chew, while others did craftworks. Some women prayed and chanted, or whatever they called it, but the majority had stomach cramps at some point. I sometimes assisted my little helper with one of the officers who dispersed Midol on the side. It was a frequently demanded item on the compound. The weak aspirin given to the women, who'd gone regularly to the nurse's station with different ailments, wasn't working for the ladies.

I had no qualms about doing what was needed. Making a connection with a guard was an asset for a select few. Every nationality had at least one to thirty women well represented inside. The Thai women outnumbered all of us by the hundreds. It was the crabs in the barrel mentality. There were many favors that couldn't be bought because of language barriers. One was trust. Most of the officer's knew a little broken English. Some were better at it than others, if they were educated. Proper schooling wasn't a prerequisite for their type of job.

"Get up now! You can't fight a court case by dreaming, Kim Hood," she yelled. It was Khun

Jillawone. She was one of the younger Khun's. For some reason a majority of these guards, would address us by our first and last names. "Okay," I said, "No yelling this early in the morning." The officers had to be dealt with in a certain kind of way, or they'd run all over us.

The punishments doled out to their own people and against women whose countries didn't have transfer treaties had no bounds. Making them kneel when they spoke to them or yelling in their faces was an everyday occurrence. Forcing them to massage their feet or hitting them randomly with short bamboo sticks was a constant. Basically, they were running them around the grounds at their leisure like flunkies. It was overlooked by the warden and permitted to carry on.

That type of behavior was unacceptable against the inmates who had a real government. It caused the officers to both admire and detest us. The Americans weren't the only ones to have a treaty with Thailand. There were at least three other countries who had working governments. The Thai's perceived it as having special protection. Really, the bottom line was we weren't the authorities over anything. They held the keys to the henhouse. Regrettably, I would come to find out no inmate was exempt from their reindeer games.

The Khun said, "Not much time to waste this morning. You have business today and will be called over the intercom early!" I'd already been informed via a letter from my appointed Thai lawyer about the upcoming trial docket. I was well prepared after waiting for a longtime already. Their courts of justice were different from the western culture. We were put in jail for a couple of days after arrest, then immediately escorted into prison. After a slow process, we were called in randomly for dates to court.

"I'm moving Khun ka," I slowly murmured. No reply was needed though. She had already moved on quickly to the next floor.

I rose from my makeshift pallet slowly. It was made out of several towels I'd bought from Nomee. She was a Thai inmate who spoke English. Nomee worked in the sewing factory and made all of my clothes, since we had to furnish them for ourselves. The uniform required was a shirt and sarong. Most foreigners bent the rules, and we wore shorts when we could. She did my laundry too and made a few of my evening meals.

She also completed a few other odd jobs for me. A minimal amount of supplies and toiletries was the payment requested monthly. There were dozens of illiterate hill-tribes women, who had no outside help. They clung to the foreigners for their livelihood, whenever the opportunity came about. Toilet paper was a luxury item for them. A lady from New Zealand called her Thai helper a lifesaver. It was a functionality of the running system. It wasn't the length of time one had already done. The determining factor for the hierarchies was solely based upon money.

I strode the six paces to the doorway like nothing special was going on. Having to start each day getting into self-preservation mode was essential. Some of the vultures on the compound cared little about anyone's court situation. We were all living in a soap opera type of existence, because of circumstances. Everyone reacted to it differently. I had to find an open shower, get dressed, rush to the bakery, grab a spot to eat, and be ready to go, all before transportation arrived. When I walked down the flight of stairs every morning, tactical maneuvers were being made mentally. Before my feet hit the last few steps, I was preparing for Lard Yao's torture. My experiences from combat training were unrivaled.

I'd applied the same boundaries and structures of military life to my current living conditions. Being aesthetically pleasing and somewhat quiet helped. Several of my fellow inmates were harmless, while others were walking black widows. The guard's attitudes were determined by the fluctuations in their personal lives. They gossiped unprofessionally with inmate's every day, like no one would ever tell.

The green jalopy used to drive us to our appointments was old, and the wheels seemed wobbly. The guards would chuckle whenever we went slightly airborne after hitting a pothole in the road. This was the only time we usually saw the male officers. It was either during the lengthy transporting of inmates to court, or whenever there was an official function inside. They would always need more security when the monks visited or the king's family.

Breathing in the polluted air was as humiliating, as the glares beaming in from the people passing by. The heavy traffic somehow managed to flow. There was nowhere to hide in the truck bed, even if I'd wanted to, with three Thai women riding alongside of me. They were going to their own court proceedings. The canopy flapped loosely with the drafty wind. Helpless hot waves of feeling like a cornered lioness, unable to pick the lock on a faulty door and jump out to my escape, consumed my thoughts briefly.

No handcuffs for restraint were used. It was too much work for them to hassle with. They had several rifles though, so definitely they weren't concerned about any of us leaping out of the back. Looking up over my shoulder, staring into the sea foam clouds, and cerulean sky, allowed my mind to wander away to a different time, and much better place.

I was met outside of the courthouse by my lawyer's representative. She made a quick introduction and asked, "Do you want to go into the briefing area with your barrister and me?" I responded quickly, "Yes, ma'am, I do." My arraignment was scheduled for morning court, I was told. We'd arrived with plenty of time to spare. Mr. Phi, who was my lawyer, along with his assistant had the guards lead us into a conference room before the hearing. He made a slight introduction sitting directly across from me, and briefly filled me in on what to expect during the proceedings.

He would not be addressed as my lawyer, but as a barrister. His translation skills would be used on my behalf. Going between me and the court as my spokesperson was standard practice. The trial would be conducted in the Thai's language only. He had submitted my discovery packet to the proper channels. All of my character reference letters from family, schoolmates, military associates, and friends had all been included.

One thing that was a commonality amongst all of the judges, was a show no mercy attitude. I understood the probable outcome, but final sentencing wouldn't be for a while. There were various layers to their judicial system before a verdict was rendered. This was a drug case involving several kilos of heroin I was caught attempting to smuggle. All of the judges were personally appointed by His Majesty the king, which was duly noted.

"Kim, I've been hired by one of your family members to defend you, but there's one off the record question I have to ask before we appear together in court." "Ok, go ahead and ask," I said to him. My eyes tightened in anticipation. Mr. Phi then proceeded to open a manila envelope and take out a spreadsheet sliding it across the table to me. He began hastily talking about different reports he'd read. They both wanted to know if I was on the run. The barrister was asking about an act of self-defense committed in 1993.

I slid my hand across the maple table, feeling its smoothness. Silently I wondered if the information he'd so proudly gathered was extracted from a Reuter's article or from another news agency. Mixing together a short, honest answer, without any type of attitude, would definitely be trying. Having my face splashed across the news outlets and airwaves wasn't something I had ever aspired to, in the secular way. It had happened only a few hours after my arrest in Thailand. My family contacted the local authorities after they were told by one of my relatives, who'd seen the CNN news footage.

After glancing over the document, I explained to him my involvement in the fatal confrontation with an abusive man. A guy, whom I would later find out had a laundry list of previous arrests and drunken outbursts. He'd thrown a Molotov cocktail underneath my car, subsequently burning it up, and his ex-wife's vehicle, too. Knocking over garbage cans, and breaking our porch light bulbs, plus a few other late-night acts. He would phone us dozens of times in a day, bragging about it all, and terrorizing the children. His threatening calls were recorded on an answering machine. That carried on for several months after the destructive burning of our vehicles, which only further provoked the situation. We took him to court, and he was convicted of communications harassment.

Still he wouldn't stop stalking us until he came armed with a brick late one night. Then his premeditated attack was carried out. I put an end to all of the danger we'd been going through with him after his brutal assault against my skull. The blow to my head, which had almost knocked me unconscious, was the breaking point on the night of our final dispute.

After waiting for so long for a trial date, I'd decided to take someone up on an offer for an all-expenses paid trip out of the country. I wasn't guilty of anything other than defending myself, but some of his relatives would frequently complain to any police officer they would see out in the streets. Telling them I was with his ex-spouse, and while he'd only had a brick, I had used a handgun.

I'd taken a bold stance when the grand jury had decided to indict me. Formalities, I was told. Against most people any heavy object used with force and venom can be a form of a weapon. There was no understanding their logic, especially since it was an ongoing reported domestic dispute. It was Alabama, so I had a good idea as to why they were being slow, in handling the case.

Several months were spent twiddling my thumbs and worrying after being put on administrative leave by the U. S. Postal Service. After continuously waiting around, to no avail for a trial date, I left town because I wanted to. There was some hesitation, but I'd visited someone in Texas for almost a week, six months prior. I was able to make it back to Alabama safely after the trip, and my lawyer didn't even miss me. When you have no bad intentions, your mind doesn't think about trouble coming around a corner.

So, being blindly free-spirited, I travelled with someone who had a rendezvous with a heroin dealer. I found myself literally pushed into a drug runner's scenario, which happened a few days into the trip.

There were some botched plans. Circumstances with my companion instantly made it an ill-fated trip for me.

If I wanted a ticket back to North America, I had to be an accomplice. There was a queasy feeling. That, perhaps, was the designed blueprint to use us both from the start. It was collectively well over thirteen kilos seized. Surely, they'd already known how many people it took to handle so much weight. They probably knew it down to the last crumb.

I could go on with the details for days with my lawyer. I'd told him that it wouldn't change the fact I was caught red handed for something just as unfathomable in his country. No matter the reason behind it, entering a plea of guilty to the trafficking charge was the only thing worth discussing. The two exchanged a glance, and the unfurling of his eyebrows suggested Mr. Phi seemed satisfied by my explanation. He then stated it was time for us to go inside of the courtroom. We quickly exited through the door and headed down the corridor.

Passing by one of the judge's chambers, the door was propped open. The secretary inside gave a seemingly knowing look. Another assumption though, because they never really knew everything like they thought. Out of the hundreds of women I'd met so far, three of them were completely innocent. They had an unfortunate blow. All were found guilty regardless of their testimonies or witnesses. Someone planting illegal substances in our belongings without us willingly participating in the plan didn't matter in the legal system.

The sunlight streaking in from the window panes lit up the courtroom, as did the flashing bulbs from the reporters in the back row. I'd sat down softly in a wooden chair, behind a table my counsel had directed me toward. There were a few low murmurs, going on throughout the room. Once what I perceived to be the bailiff, called the court to order everyone fell silent, and we all stood up. Three male judges walked in and sat down like a panel. All were dressed in the same black robes, and white shirts except for the one in the middle. He was distinguishable by a lapel adorning his attire.

After we'd all took our seats, and the process had started, everything went by in a blur. Not understanding a single word being spoken, I was constantly glancing at my barrister for some type of acknowledgement about what was being said. He would only address the judge. His head frequently turned and nodded at me for reassurance.

On the ride back to Lard Yao, all I could do was replay in my mind, the unusual sequence of events which transpired inside of the courtroom. All of the inmates were allowed to be fed before leaving from court or briefly visit with their families. My counsel had bought us some food from one of the carts that aligned the outside of the courthouse parking lot. They led me back into the room, where we'd been earlier before the trial. I was a little anxious about needing a debriefing, but I also knew how and when to stay quiet. Before we sat down to eat, my barrister's assistant gave me a hug. Immediately, everything seemed odd, but the words spoken next explained her reaction.

I then knew there wouldn't be any coming back to second, or third court for any type of appeals. I was sentenced to sixty-five years in the first court, which was astonishing. It was going to make news for a drug case. Everyone until that point had been given either a sentence of life or death by way of beheading in first court. It took months and sometimes years of waiting for an appeal of reduction or a king's pardon. For some reason the courts had used sagacity, and not prolonged my case.

The amount of letters my barrister had received from my past military commanders and fellow soldiers impressed them, I was told. The ruling also meant coming into play would be the U. S. Transfer Treaty. It was due to the efforts from the U. S. Attorney General, the U. S. Government, and the king, who'd signed an agreement between the two countries.

Therefore, I would be eligible for transport to a U.S. federal institution. It would be as close to my home of residence as possible, after serving a completion of four years, because of the numbered sentence I'd received. Hopefully, I wouldn't have to face too many leftover repercussions, because of jumping bond. If I'd been given a life sentence, which several Americans had been stuck with, I would've been required to complete an eight-year stint.

The ladies on the compound always looked for some reason to hang out together briefly on the weekends. They would definitely celebrate that hurdle. We sometimes allowed other countries to join in on our activities. There was an unspoken strength within the numbers. It was beneficial for them to befriend us, whether they were from South Africa or Uzbek. Holidays, birthdays, family emergencies, meetings, or whatever was going on with any of them, we were there for each other in some form.

It was a relief to be arriving back at the compound late. I could process everything alone before telling anybody else. Everyone had usually come back glum and depressed, after their first court appearance, but we all supported each other with positivity regardless, except for the vile ones. They didn't care about us nor themselves.

Mr. Phi seemed very happy while explaining all of the details, but I was more stunned than elated. Because of the dismal conditions, time served in a foreign prison was considered double punishment, but at least I had a tentative release date for getting out of the jungle from hell. One thing the courts had mandated was for me to get a physical. I'd refused to go inside of the creepy, haunted looking hospital upon first arriving at Lard Yao.

I didn't need any medical attention at the time and didn't want them evaluating anything on my body. I agreed to get one completed as soon as the new day dawned. I had a few issues over the last few months, a doctor could fix, like my frequent migraines and reoccurring abdominal problems. I thanked both of my counsels. There was solace in knowing, that was the first and last time I'd ever be meeting with them.

"Reo khao." he said. "You quickly get out!" Listening to the khun of transportation, using a mix of Thai and English combined together was not amusing after a long day, and at that late time of night. The shining, oversized bright spotlight sitting atop the concrete wall along the entranceway told us why we had stopped and where we were.

I always moved around at my own pace. Even in the midst of my most trying times, I wasn't quite sure why it was a part of my personality. It seemed as if it couldn't be changed. I wasn't in much of a rush to willy-nilly, walk back through the door, which encased me like a herring in a rusty tin can, to then pull out a zipped, micro-fibered miniature pallet and lay down with only one small pillow. Still and all, it's what I had to do.

A number of people had straw or plastic mats. A few had tiny air mattresses, but the cost was hefty. They were confiscated regularly, so more money could be extorted by a couple of greedy officers. They turned a blind eye by allowing certain items from the parcels to slip past them and get inside of the prison grounds. The showers were turned off at a certain time each day. If we were a night shift worker or had come in from court late, we had to bathe by drawing water from one of the six long, white marble dunk tanks, which were primarily used for washing clothes. After getting cleaned up and led back into my unit for lockdown, not everyone was asleep. At least my closest ally was already sleeping.

She was an American woman from the Midwest, and she had my back totally. I had hers too. There were at least a couple of random fights daily. We had both witnessed our fair share of Thai women grouping together, to gang jump on farangs. That was a name some of the Americans were called by the locals.

A few of the foreigners were desperate to view television at lockdown. During the weeknights they would willingly sit up for several hours, watching Thai programming. I couldn't do it. I didn't want to learn much of the language, except for the basics. Neither did I want to work for or become too at ease around any of them. My saving grace to maintaining my sanity was books and magazines. We were allowed as many of them as we wanted if they could fit into our outside locker with all our other belongings.

Two magazines, and three books were all I kept inside of the room at night, but I'd cherished every one of them. Being a current events enthusiast, I was completely miserable not being able to watch any news programs at all. The subscriptions that I would receive from my family, in my parcel every other month, meant the world to me, for staying somewhat up-to-date. I appreciated the photographs, and everything else they'd sent to me immeasurably. The exercise of the mind was crucial.

I was glad my cohort had already spread out my homemade sleeping mat. Sitting down on my spot next to her, it was time to exhale. We were on the furthest end of the room. It was less than 30ft long with one hundred other women in it. My nightly routine was saying a prayer and composing a visual sonata of memories from my past while trying to block out the background noises.

My anamnesis was full of recollections of a prior life filled with adventures, mementos, and fulfillment. I'd tossed my career out of the window because of not one, but two felony charges. I'd only heard about dysfunctional youths with tattoos, and high school drop-outs, getting into trouble. It was unbeknownst to me how his type of living situation became my fate.

Participating in the girl scouts, piano lessons, church choir, debutantes' ball, ROTC, and organized sports hadn't been a deterrent. Having a two-parent home, loving siblings, family vacations, birthday parties, tight-knit relatives, cars, money, the United States Army, the United States Post Office, accolades, popularity, and relationships galore, should've been enough to have kept me steady.

I'd been on the right path in life after getting baptized at a young age, but something had drastically changed. There are certain people who get an untouchable confidence, when they think having a little bit of charisma and being whip-smart can keep anything detrimental from happening to them. I'd fell into that category unfortunately. Now I was paying for it dearly.

I could never fall off to sleep easily in Lard Yao. Even after writing long letters. With no outside distractions to make me feel tired, it made the nights extra-long. Sleeping almost directly beneath one of the three, large ceiling fans that hung overhead, I'd watch the palmetto leaf shaped blades whirl around every evening to become drowsy. When idly gazing or reading didn't work, I had another trick. Thinking about all of the fun days and cool nights, I'd once experienced as a young sergeant, would oftentimes be the only thing to relax me.

It was back during a two-year duty stop at the 731st Military Intelligence Battalion Kunia, when I was stationed at Schofield Barracks, Hawaii. I felt a sense of pride while walking through the expansive, underground tunnel. When work time was over with, there were many hours spent hanging off post with friends and enjoying the breathtaking cities on the Island of Oahu, from 1989 to 1991. On countless occasions, I'd free dived in Waianae with the spinner dolphins, or snorkeled throughout the waters of Honolulu, and leisurely explored the colorful, ocean panoramas of underwater sea life like it was an aquarium. Twice, within a few feet away from me, a couple of enormous, green sea turtles swam past without incident. It was a privilege to have enough available time to learn how to kayak while navigating around the beaches. Making the adventures even more enticing was following the path of the thousands of native Hawaiian royalty, who'd once frolicked along those same coastlands. Whenever it was possible, my friends and I would end most evenings sliding unbothered into ongoing imu pit luaus, for an authentic feast. Those events always made the nights end perfectly. I'd once tried fly fishing, which I disliked. Making up for it was not hard, after finding a beach with gritty grains of warm, beige sand surrounding the city of Kailua.

Several times I'd hiked past a bamboo trail, all the way up the rickety, Haiku stairway to Heaven. With its worn, sturdy railings, and rusty, narrow metal steps, the physical challenge made climbing up the scenic viewing spot dangerous but rewarding. Whether it was daytime or under the cover of darkness, it was awe-inspiring. However, there was no experience better than my discreet, isolated gem of a beach. It was a small one, and not even a mile long. Some of my Samoan friends had shown it to me around by the windward coast. We'd play volleyball on the creamy white, fine powdery sand which felt like smooth, confectionary sugar to the touch. Afterwards, leisurely rinsing off in the surrounding azure waters while floating around on small boogie boards was absolutely relaxing.

There was once an event which had me wanting to settle down and get married. It was something about the romantic setting. I'd served as a maid of honor at an open-air wedding on a beach in Waikiki. Later on, in that same evening, I was fortunate enough to witness an elaborate reception, at a hotel restaurant which held a three-story aquarium with divers in it. There were many other occasions when I'd take a quick helicopter flight for the weekend over to the tropical island of paradise, which was Maui. Several sunrise outings were spent paddling my koa wood canoe leisurely around, with over one-hundred miles of beaches to choose from, bordering along the vast coastline of Kihei.

I was cooling off in the afternoons with tandem paragliding rides over Makawao city. Elevated thousands of feet above ground while soaring high in the air over the mountaintops, inactive volcanoes, and clouds, with a circular rainbow sometimes following directly underneath us, was a natural high.

Some days were spent taking pictures while carefully navigating slippery, narrow trails, down to the rocky, burnt red sand beach in Hana. The tall, black lava cliffs were beautifully silhouetted against its stunning, turquoise sea. Later on, in the evenings we'd take a ride on a glass bottom boat, a dinner cruise. Oftentimes it was to a turtle sanctuary, as tiger sharks, schools of tuna, and brightly spotted opah moonfish swam underneath the tranquil waters for our entertainment.

I would eventually take a flight back over to my isle of residence to go joyriding along the north shores on a Sunday night. I would slowly scan the tourist sections for some action or go into any one of the several, non-stop night clubs, occasionally free of charge. There were many impulsive instances on breezy nights. I would cruise towards the strong fragrances which were permeating the crisp air, surrounding certain parts of the island.

Carefully venturing past the few wooden fences and signs on the Dole Pineapple Fields was not difficult. I was chilling out with my significant other underneath the glow of the moonlight and stars and smelling the sweet aromas while in the most remote areas of the plantation. With so many acres upon acres off limits, sitting on the berm next to the red clay dirt road was never anything more than an innocent adrenaline rush.

Those were the memories that sustained me. All I wanted to think of, while lying on the floor in my cell, was one of my many dangerous, outdoors excursions. Not too many miles away from my barracks were winding, hiking trails to be mastered and mountain ranges to climb up. There were several different flowing waterfalls to view also along its pathways. The rugged, untamed woodland would always give me a challenging workout as I carefully passed over its towering velvety green, fluted cliffs and blooming flowers.

Climbing across the steep ridges, coming up from any one of the many vast rainforests, in the valleys of Oahu with a backpack on, was not an adventure for the fainthearted. Slowly contouring along the crumbly, loose rocks, gorges, strawberry guava trees, and tangled thickets that I'd trekked, led to the summit of my favorite mountainous region. That was where a one-of-a-kind phenomenon stood. The locals called it the

Upside Down Falls. It was a worthwhile hike to simply enjoy the unique beauty.

After reaching the peak and sliding out onto the slippery edge of the cliff, my best friend and I would peer over to watch the cascading water pound the perfect depth of river below. The tourists looking from the only scenic point in the deep valley below or along the crest of the Old Pali Highway shoulder was always enjoying the views. Sightseers watched in amazement at our fearlessness to shimmy so close and dangle our feet out across the side of the ledge. Being the only two sun-kissed, caramel colored people in the vicinity on my nature jaunts always stood out. Not a lot of ethnic people were into an outdoorsy type of lifestyle.

I never worried about the distances travelled. I'd hit almost all four corners of the world. Also being fortunate to have been an enlisted soldier during a time in which we were still able to take a free hop on a plane anywhere, only when there were available openings, and normally that was the case.

I was always taking full advantage of being young, childfree, and enjoying the journeys. The attraction to one of the most demanding, hiking regions on the island was what one of the waterfalls could perform. When there were strong winds swirling around in the area after coinciding with any heavy downpours of rain, the magic would soon begin.

The aerated waters would continuously blow back up, as if in a circle, with a cool, light mist gently washing over our faces, and it was invigorating. One night we'd made our way up the mountainside after a long midnight hike. We watched a rainbow form in the darkness. It was halfway between the top of the waterfall and the bowl-shaped basin below. The colors weren't bright like the ones I'd seen in the daytime. They were a white and grey mixture, but seeing something like that with misty rain falling was enchanting.

Reluctantly my mind was pulled back into prison by listening to the relentless chorus of nighttime pitter-patter and faint footsteps. It ruined my train of thought. Random women constantly walking to the bathroom area, always made me think about what a refugee camp must be like. Since the pictures I'd viewed in magazines resembled the life I was now experiencing. Their oppression was horrific, and they didn't have a choice in what had befallen them.

Dangerous choices had been made by the majority of us who now found ourselves incarcerated. Some of the ladies couldn't take it. They were either popping pills or staying up late looking shell-shocked. There were a few Thais who always came back into Lard Yao because living on the streets of Thailand was considerably worse than being locked away.

The rooms were not large at all. On one end up a couple of steps behind a low, cinder block wall were several choices of empty holes in the tile floor, which were used like a toilet. Every twenty minutes someone monitoring with a splashing, bucket of water drawn from a trough, would ensure all of the effluent was properly flushed down the drain. It was swept out to the dreaded, stinking moat.

Any beautiful distraction I could muster up in Lard Yao at nighttime was better than the alternative. There were other inmates who had no prior exciting life from before, in which to help guide them through the maze. Having no other option, but to try and be on top of my game to the highest degree ever in my life, was a daily agenda. However, there was a strange bonding, with people who normally would've never been in the realm of my inner circle. The time I'd spent encouraging a few of the inmates to keep the faith, had more of an impact on certain women than initially thought. That was something I could not have foreseen, even with a crystal ball.

HOSPITAL REJECT TEA

"Hey Kim, Tangelo asked, you're moving fast this morning, where're you rushing to?" "I've got to get a complete physical at the infirmary, I said. If I get some extra time later, we'll catch up." "Well, she said, I've got to tell you about what happened to the possessed chick when you were away at court. After lights out, she started howling and climbing up the bars like a monkey, babbling incoherently!"

We conversed for a few moments about how many women were being affected by sleep deprivation, the latest madness going on inside of Lard Yao's walls. They would have the monks come in and perform a type of spiritual cleanse on her within weeks if she didn't pull herself together.

Tangelo was one of the busiest Americans. I'd become relatively close to her inside of Lard Yao. We'd arrived in the same year and had clicked on a few levels conversation wise. I didn't get to hang out with her too often, once she'd learned to speak fluent Thai. She'd gotten a job at the bakery to help pass her time away. She worked hard for the compound, which was something I wasn't even remotely interested in ever doing. I disliked the innocuous gossip about other people's personal breakdowns, but it happened so frequently. Someone would just snap, and everyone couldn't stop talking about who was probably next.

There was inner trepidation about the Thai personnel, who were working inside of the hospital. I was glad to see a nurse smiling while standing inside of the dispensary window. I walked slowly on the sidewalk. It felt weird going to a jungle hospital for anything at all. She held a clipboard in one hand and a pen in the other. "Sawatdee ka," she said quickly. I knew that was the greeting the Thai's used when meeting someone, but I feigned ignorance to all parts of their language. "I don't speak Thai, but I need to see a doctor as a walk-in patient." She had me sign in and handed me a form to fill out. Then she pointed to three sets of metal benches in front of the only entrance, where several women were already seated.

I had a choice of sitting with the Thai's on the first one or on the second set with a couple of Rhodesians, but I chose the last bench where the Nigerians were. Making that decision had seemed like a no-brainer, but ironically during the passing hours that I sat chatting with them before my name was called, quickly became detrimental mentally. The information that those ladies had begun sharing with me would become a major spark in plummeting me headfirst towards a course of blinding revenge.

"Kim Hood, you come now," the nurse said. The constant sounds of broken English were like nails on a chalkboard to my ears, but I was relieved to finally be summoned. After following behind her through the door, there was a vestibule with a small room on one side where an intake exam was performed, and then I was walked through the ward. In a section of the corridor there were thin, white sheets draped overhead like curtains, from the wall to the middle of the hallway, blocking the view of the patients. I could faintly see through the sheets, enough to determine that they were laying on small cots, and not the floor.

It was a drab building with no visible windows. A strong scent of tiger balm was in the air. I was then guided to another room to wait for the doctor. Looking around the room and up along the walls were two letters of certification, and one was from England. After about twenty minutes, a demure looking Asian man of medium height came in, and I was inherently impressed by his introduction. He spoke eloquently with a slight accent, and lucky for me there wouldn't be any type of communication barrier. I described to him the ailments that I'd started having since being in Lard Yao, and he seemed to annotate everything down on a sheet of paper.

Once I finished talking, he put on a pair of gloves and opened up a cabinet. He took out a large container filled with cotton balls. The doctor then opened a mini-sized refrigerator and took out a medium sized jar full of cloudy, brown liquid. After squeezing some of it into a small, plastic medical dropper that he'd also taken out, he put the tubular vial and a couple of cotton balls inside of a tiny plastic bag. "Take this," he said. "It will make your stomach and headache pains go away. Squeeze one milliliter of fluid into your mouth periodically during the day and discard any remnants before lockdown."

I asked about the medication, but the name was weird sounding. I'd never heard of it. He stated it was similar to ayahuasca tea, and he'd made a fresh batch at least twice a month. The foraged materials used were from certain plant roots, leaves, and slivers from various barks gathered by the prison orderlies. It all came from the vegetation and saplings in the back area of the hospital. Taking a holistic approach towards health, whenever the situation permitted, was what he always practiced according to him. Some of the inmates were only willing to take synthetic pills.

A couple of leaves floating around the top of the jar and wondered how well they strained the brewed mixture, but that wasn't making me too leery. Being a naturalist and frequent abdominal pains were the reasons I'd decided to accept the tonic. How the concoction was going to be the remedy for two separate medical issues was lingering in the back of my mind, nonetheless. After spending most of the day at the hospital, I thanked the doctor. Hurriedly, I got out of there and back onto the prison grounds.

Traversing the compound after the work factories had let out for the day was similar to a truck driver being stuck in a traffic jam. I could see over the top of all of the short women but moving past them was a futile effort. They were everywhere. I always referred to it as organized chaos time. The guards were in the shacks standing around in the shade, in the back corners of the factories. They were somewhere observing and getting a massage or working behind a desk. Some of them would look out at us, but we truly were not monitored as tightly. When fights broke out, the Khun's did manage to get there pretty quickly. They were running in low heels, and skirts with sticks and were intimidating to most.

I knew my dinner meal was waiting for me, whenever I could get to it. My dependable, Thai helper, my special friend from New York, would have something prepared. Her name was Irene. She'd learned how to speak the Thai's language and prepare their food, too. Nobody ate in the Gongolian if they could afford not to.

"There are two bowls of Kee Mao left and a bag of sticky rice for the durian," Nomee said.

I'd always made her feel appreciated, regardless of what dishes she created. The pungent smelling, sweet, creamy fruit was so hard to get; I never passed up on the garlicky almond and pineapple custard, exotic taste of durians. It was definitely unfair that the Thai's and Africans had a hookup with access to the kitchen. They blatantly had a hustle going on. They needed a way of making money but never having any American food, or letting us into the kitchen was unfair.

Even the meals that visitors sent in could only be from orders, thru the Lanka store. We were allowed a cold hamburger and fries every other week, which were purchased by the missionaries we paid. Holiday spreads were authorized on certain occasions. They were sent in for free by the missionaries or Consulate personnel. No food items such as steaks, pork chops, crab legs, pizza, lobster, mashed potatoes, sausages, bacon, hotdogs, cornbread, waffles, bologna, rolls, grapes, strawberries, oranges, apples, watermelons, or kiwi. Nothing close to what's considered palatable to an American was available.

We had all settled into the pattern of paying for glass noodles, Pad Thai with peanuts, lychees, and mangosteens, or something similar to that week after week. When fried chicken would hit the black market, but it was double coated in egg wash and dredged in rice flour, it was cooked so hard it was laughable, but we would buy one leg apiece because it was all we were able to order. "Give me the bag of durian and sticky rice. I'll see you tomorrow," I said. The taste from the tea I was randomly shooting into my mouth was bitter but tolerable. I'd almost finished it and needed to go take a quick shower before the water was turned off because the day was almost over.

Shortly after my head hit the pillow, after evening lockdown, trouble quickly arrived. My abdomen started rumbling, and I was in excruciating pain. I was almost running behind the low wall in the room to one of the banal holes in the floor within minutes, up and down constantly with everyone staring, and it was progressively getting worse. Most of the American women were scattered about in different buildings, but five of them slept in my section. They were all sitting around in my cramped corner of the room trying to figure out what was wrong with me.

I had a slight fever, chills, diarrhea, and felt my stomach retching, but it wouldn't come up. I was grateful since too much was going on already. I told them what the doctor had given me. After telling them about what I'd eaten earlier, they automatically blamed the Thai doctor. My illness continued throughout the night as they wet rags and wiped my forehead. One of them rubbed my abdominal area, which was awkward, but it happened because I needed tending to.

As time wore on, I started to drift off to sleep from sheer exhaustion. There'd been a lunch invitation from a couple of the Nigerian ladies whom I'd met earlier that day. Definitely, I didn't want to miss that. Knowing their attitudes, they wouldn't want to invite me again. I hadn't really felt comfortable socializing with them before like a few of the other foreigners had been doing. Some of them were loud and boisterous. They seemed to get into an argument with each other, a Thai inmate or a Khun, every day without fail. I was thinking about the homebrewed tea as sleepiness started taking over. I also wondered what the heck had those stupid, cotton balls supposed to have been used for.

I woke up at dawn to the sounds of muffled chanting. Leaning up to survey the room, there was a minimum of about fifteen Thai's already up. Lying back down on my pillow was useless. Several devout women began their days with a Buddhist ritual before most of us were even awake. My concern was not about their morning activity but how my body doing. In actuality, once I started moving, it felt great. At some point during the night, I recall a couple of the Thai's coming over to my bedding and voicing their opinions about what was making me sick.

From what I'd gathered, which wasn't lost in translation, they said it must've been the durian. Even though I'd eaten it a few times before, in the past it had caused adverse reactions in certain people. They'd been eating the fruit since childhood supposedly and even touted it as having some aphrodisiac effects. Whatever the culprit had been was inconsequential to me now, after all the pain and suffering. I was glad it was over and relieved to still be amongst the population.

NEFARIOUS NIGERIAN NEIGHBORS

My initial shock of being surrounded by such a large group of Nigerians wasn't surprising. The uneasy feeling quickly dissipated, after a couple of them encouraged me to come and sit down with them. There were at least ten of them, sitting on plastic mats in a perfectly shaded spot behind one of the buildings with a lookout standing next to the corner lockers. They had several courses to choose from. Spicy goat stew, with a visible layer of oil floating around the top, jollof rice, smashed spaghetti balls, okra salsa, and whole pieces of fried fish with the eyes and scales still attached. They also had fried plantains for dessert and the aromatic smell in the air of rambutans and jackfruit, which were in a bowl of watery ice.

Not waiting for me to make the first move, one of them got up and started dipping food into her bowl. Then everyone else got in the line following suit. There was no desire to test my stomach by putting anything else into it, which could potentially send me reeling again. Being rude wasn't on the agenda either. Gingerly eating a small portion of the rice and some fruit was satisfactory. The cuisine wasn't the reason why I'd come into their space anyways. I needed to gather more information about the Nigerian woman responsible for the organization of the bungled drug fiasco which had landed me in such a terribly, retched place.

One of the Nigerian ladies asked me, "Had you ever considered the possibility one day you'd be locked away in a foreign prison?" "Of course not, who would?" "Okay, she said slowly, but your case had a co-defendant in it, right?" Right then, I'd been asked one question too many. That was going to be par for the course. I knew conversations would be coming several different ways until every ounce of information from that group of women was gained. "I noticed that the majority of your people work for the compound, why is that?" I asked.

The visible leader of their group went on to tell me why some subjected themselves to the menial pay and mental torture of factory work, considering that it was voluntary for foreigners. Since their government didn't have the funds to help them, they were willing to work for pennies. There were some other details about the Nigerians survival inside of Lard Yao, which was shared with me also.

I was happy to sway the dialogue from the start. That was the beginning of several more upcoming days of meals together. I made it a priority to speak every day with at least one of them but not in a malicious way. It was out of necessity. One thing I should've asked, but didn't, was why they had three hungry cats roaming around freely where the food was prepared.

The sequence of events for the following months were spent becoming somewhat close with the most gossipy yet educated Nigerian women. There are no orderly account. So many days were mixed together, being on constant alert alongside the recent revelations of how hard Nigerian drug dealers had worked to find mules. These were the days before internet search engines had taken an emotional toll. Learning about the luring of Americans on trips with promises of easy cash was information overload. Knowing they'd been fully aware of the fact that it had ruined the lives of so many of their own countrymen made the punch even more devastating.

The Nigerians' words dripped with a vitriolic tone when discussing their co-conspirators. Supposedly they were running around stress free in the city of Chicago. They had intimate knowledge about the orchestrators behind the debacle, which we'd all walked right into.

It stunned me; I could literally feel the anger seeping in slowly. That was something I hadn't felt about my case prior to my newfound knowledge of the international games, which had been so recklessly played. Anger was causing certain thoughts of mine to become increasingly animated like a dark sheath stretching out with a desire to avenge.

I'm unsure as to why one of their kittens decided to follow me. The more I tried to push it away, it seemed determined to keep coming back. It'd started walking around my legs and rubbing up against me. There were several cats and kittens on the compound. The Thai's took good care of the majority of them. The only other women who'd cared for the cats either had no friends or were just lonely animal lovers.

There were at least a couple of Americans who had one. Ever since I'd gotten close to the Nigerians, something seemed to always pop up. After a couple of weeks of mingling with them, one of their animals was now clinging to me. It had odd eyes with one blue and the other green, but it wasn't creepy.

As soon as the new day came around, he would trot out from behind a building, eventually finding me. Once my attention was won over, my associates found it humorous I'd named the animal Marko. I'd started taking care of him. In the ensuing months, I'd built my days around feeding him when he came out, which wasn't often. The cats seemed to retreat and come out from behind a bush or tree at different times. If I'd written home and said I lived in a virtual zoo, they would've thought I'd succumbed to drug usage myself. I was living in a somewhat jungle like existence, but I could never turn into a junkie, no matter the dilemma.

The cool season was coming. With the wind blowing down into the compound and hugging the soon to be demolished concrete walls, it was all too familiar. However, it was as if I'd woken up in a different prison. My daily routine had become a ritual of taking care of myself and Marko, but he was a no-show for the first time since he'd started eating my food. It had been about five months of me caring for him, and I'd kind of looked forward to seeing him. For two days I searched for the kitten. On the third day I'd finally questioned one of the few English-speaking Thai girls who worked on the yard detail, subsequently realizing Marko's probable fate.

"Ning Po," I said, "where have all the cats gone lately?"

"They caught a bag full of cats and released them to the outside for the prevention of overcrowding," she said.

"Did you have one, Kim?" That was something I hadn't paid attention to. The officers always had the Thai girls doing things around the grounds, and I really didn't care before. Whenever the Americans spoke about the cats running around, they were always making a joke about demons being cast into them by the monks, and I would listen and laugh. After a short conversation, I moved on and went to my hideout spot at the back end of the prison.

I could've hung out around other inmates, but everything was cast in a shadow, and I didn't want to be asked a dozen times what was wrong. There was only one person on the compound who really knew anything about me personally, but she wasn't a woman I could ever confide in. I was going through somewhat of a detachment and talking about it would've only frightened her anyway. Masking the emotional pain and internalizing it was challenging enough. Now that my Band-Aid was gone, it felt like a scab was peeled off with it and taken away too soon before the healing had progressed.

I'd become fast associates with a few of the Nigerians. All had gone well until I had to back away momentarily. One of them had passed me a lengthy screed about her previous neighbors when she lived in the Windy City. It was all about their capers, successful and otherwise, which they'd been involved in together when she was a free woman. The venom spewed was palpable. She had given me names, home, and school addresses, job locations and a plethora of detailed information only a trusted insider would be privy to. Even if I was to be given a bag of gold at the end of a rainbow, I wouldn't partake in any more tomfoolery intertwined with another individual.

Making that statement made it easy for me to stop stirring the pot, letting them know there was no hidden animosity against the people involved. I wanted to do my time and leave the situation as it was. Their feelings about whatever vindictiveness that needed to occur really wasn't anyone else's business. Tending to my kitten had been a peaceful smokescreen. Subsequently, the conversations eventually changed anyway. They were more about the predicament we were all in, and a milder tone was established.

Exasperated and falling down into a sitting position behind the Gongolian, I needed the sturdy structure to brace my weary body. My kitten was gone. I also hadn't decided if I wanted to become much closer with someone inside of Lard Yao as of yet, and it made the angst creep in also. Putting on a fierce persona was easy, because that was me even before my fall from grace, but everyone gets bored at some point. As the air backed away from my constricting lungs and tightening muscles, it was so easy to fall back into a suppressed anger. Though I'd said things were fine, that wasn't what I truly felt every day. Now, I was right back at the doorstep of a hollow darkness thinking about tethered projectiles and spirits of salt.

I hated the desire of wanting to inflict pain upon another person and her family members with long, drawn out torture. It was the eye for an eye type of personality. Though responsibility had been taken and accepted for my criminal actions, repercussions were coming for everyone else involved. The people responsible for the prison fiasco needed to be held accountable, too.

It felt as if I were a wounded bird or a trapped butterfly, enclosed inside the confines of Lard Yao. I was completely relegated behind the shady trappings from a bunch of people I didn't know much about. They didn't care about the casualties of the war on drugs, and they'd plucked away at my ranking in life. Therefore, I was left with no other choice, but one future act of retaliation.

DAYMARES

In retrospect, I should've known better, bouncing away onto an unpaved, dusty road while out on bond, even though I'd felt conflicted in doing so. Some people have to be shown what the consequence of certain actions really mean, when a didactic won't do. The most sweltering day I'd experienced in Lard Yao so far, tiny beads of sweat were popping on my face. They were rolling faster than I could wipe them away. Even underneath the shadiest of spots, we were going to be feeling the sizzling heat.

The occasional breeze coming through didn't smell like I thought it would. With such a putrid moat surrounding its perimeter, it didn't stink in certain areas either. Ironically, it was the flowing scent coming from all the flowers aligning the prison grounds. Being outside underneath a tree constantly drinking Jamba juice, or water, and wiping away salty droplets was bad enough. Going into the crowded Gongolian during the daytime would've been worst.

Anyone who didn't work and couldn't take the blazing temperatures was posted up inside of there. It was a slow, simmering madhouse I rarely joined. Only when it rained did I ever go in there or if it was too hot outside. I sat at the same bench each time, with one of my closest associates. A couple from Ghana always sat on the bench across from us, at the table on my right-hand side when we went in. We had what was called a foreigner's back wall. The Thai's knew exactly where we were going to sit when we came in. They didn't have a problem with moving. Actually, some of those Thai inmates seemed like little kids to me.

The Thai's gave us our space when we wanted it, and there were several foreigners who wouldn't work. They liked hanging out with the Thai's and intermingling with them all day. The two sitting across from me were seemingly estranged from their Ghanaian sisters. I had a serious conversational pull towards them. Being open about their lifestyle was frowned upon by the women from their country, who were antiquated in their beliefs. They'd received some harsh criticism from a few of the ladies for being together for such a lengthy amount of time.

We were cool but really only talked when inside of the Gongolian. Out on the compound we barely waved, since it was a fairly, timid relationship. The woman I had spoken with the most, between the two, was named Arumdae. She had a nihilistic view about a lot of issues. When she would condemn any type of religion, I explained to her why I'd never forsake mine for several reasons. Even when others found my denomination to be believers of nothing more than fairytales and cast pebbles at me for my mistakes, I didn't waver in my faith. Most of my thinking process, as it pertained to organized religion, had come from my mother who'd figuratively sketched a cross onto my chest.

We would have some interesting conversations while blocking out the ongoing massive heat or rain, as time passed on. I did understand Arumdae's pain somewhat. Since being locked up for so many years without a transfer treaty in the works, she'd felt hopeless about ever being free again, with her seventy-five year sentence. She'd been in Lard Yao for over twelve years, appealing her case, and hoping for a King's Pardon.

Everybody else in the Gongolian would usually have at least six on both benches with gibberish going on all day. We were virtually living like castaways. With time restraints put on us, most inmates acted territorial knowing we would soon be getting kicked outside. Being pushed back into the harsh weather at least one hour before the setup of each meal while trying to stay cool, dry, and sane every day was the procedure.

Deciding to sweat it out during the scorching hot days instead of going inside of the noisy Gongolian was a sad option. Stretching out on my blue, plastic mat in the grass underneath a tree similar to a banyan, during the latest massive heat wave, was like a punishment. However, being stuck inside the Gongolian with all of those women and the constant sounds of different languages was even more irritating, after so many days in a row of it. Choosing the lesser of the two evils normally ended with me finding a semi-quiet and partially shaded area.

As usual, I'd started daydreaming to zone out. The wistful thoughts were about an ecological tour that I'd previously taken with a couple of nature lovers. It was off the Georgia coast on Blackbeard Island, about five years before my incarceration. Clear memories from any one of my numerous travels allowed my frustrations to always be a bit more bearable inside of Lard Yao.

Thinking about how I was lying under one of the weather-beaten whitewashed, old skeletal trees along the shoreline of Boneyard Beach, without a care in the world, made my heart smile. I drank wine-coolers and did some bird watching as the cool wind blew in. There were kayakers out in the distance. My friends combing for sand dollars, instead of sea shells, while trying to navigate through an obstacle course of driftwood, made for light entertainment. The evoked feelings of nostalgia were abruptly put on hold, however, by an out of control train heading in my direction.

"Hey, Kim, one of the Khun's wants you to come to your locker," she said. "Who's calling for me?" I asked. "Come right now, she's yelling at your friend!" I ran to see what the summons was all about. No officer had ever sent one of their stooges out to look for me. As soon as I turned the corner between the buildings, the smell of a wet dog hit me. It was the known scent of the Khun, who was furiously emptying out a locker, which was not far away from mine.

It was my little helper's locker, who was just standing there, with her head hanging down. Khun Soon Moe Lee was in a rage over a small amount of orange colored pills, which had been found inside some folded papers. The Khun had been told by an inmate that she wasn't the only officer who had pain pills and muscle relaxants being passed around on the black market. She was so upset. My Thai helper and two other girls were only supposed to be working for her. I really didn't get the jest of why she was so angry.

While trying to process what was going on, another inmate handed the Khun a thick rope like material made out of cordage from the fibers of dead tree bark. She gave it to Nomee, and what happened next was beyond brutal. The young woman started hitting her own legs, arms, and back, literally punishing herself! I'd never seen such self-inflicted punishment up close, but I'd heard about flagellation before.

The Khun seemed to have a grin on her face, when looking over at me and the other inmate. I was caught off guard by that style of punishment, and realized the officer was trying to prove a point to us about who was in charge, but I wasn't feeling it at all. The cumulative impact of all the ruminating I'd been doing over the past few months caused an opposite effect. It was probably intended to lead me further away from who I really was. In actuality, it had become a force in helping to turn me back around.

The young lady, who'd been helping me out for the past couple of years was docile, sweet and undeserving of what was happening to such a high degree of pain. She was only incarcerated for stealing food for her baby and was given a completely unfair sentence for such a small crime. She was barely nineteen while I was twenty-eight at the time. Why she'd allowed the officer to break her down was understandable though because Thai inmates always cowered down when the Khun's wanted them to. As soon as skin was broken and a trickle of blood started to run down her leg, I'd realized the depths of idiocy had a stopping point. When you teeter on the verge of a total moral collapse, you can change the outcome if you really want to.

I was compelled to attempt one of the most dangerous things I could do in a dilemma. Boldly, I stepped right into harm's way and dealt with someone else's problem. It's a crazy trait to have, but I'd felt the need to diffuse the situation. Reaching out, I grabbed her hand to stop her from hitting herself.

"Come on Nomee, and drop the damn rope," I softly said.

There was no way I was going to let the sadistic Khun get off by watching such a heinous act being carried out over some pills. We weren't supposed to have them anyways. One glance over at the Khun, and I could tell she was seething. She was in utter disbelief as we started to walk away. It felt sort of good though. I'd blatantly stood up for someone who had nothing to give me in return but her appreciation.

Sympathy for a Thai woman while in Lard Yao was something I couldn't've imagined ever happening. Unbeknownst to me at the time, the incident would become the main catalyst behind saving my mother a boatload of future tears.

It was like a natural act of compassion, which was what I'd felt towards a lot of people in need, deep inside of my soul. It was the right thing to do because the girl was fearful of standing up for herself. I could hear the Khun shout as we were leaving, "Kim Hood, what are you doing?" she yelled.

I kept the pace brisk while we headed back to the central most part of the prison. We both were calm and thankful the Khun's voice was becoming a distant echo. I knew it would've been bad if she'd tried to exact harm upon me. My mind was immediately made up. If the worst-case scenario happened, I'd unfortunately be forced to introduce her to the art of the rough and tumble. Therefore, giving her the comeuppance, she so desperately deserved. Fortunately, she didn't make a move to detain me. Not all monsters spit fire. Some of them only blow smoke.

Being vigilant after a few years of being locked away, inside of Lard Yao, easily revealed the daily work cycle of the officers. It never really alternated. The only time there was any type of unwanted excitement was when there was a fight, stabbing, sickness, death, water pressure problems, or visits from outside dignitaries. Whenever the king or his people would come through and ask questions, the Khun's made it clear to be polite. Don't look into their eyes, and definitely don't say anything unless forced to. Sometimes a couple of the ladies would be bold, speaking out against any injustices they'd perceived. When the unspoken rules were broken, they always punished those women immediately, making it appear to be all for not. Nothing ever changed for the better.

A monumental assemblage was put together during the late-nineties in preparation for certain members of the royal family. There was to be an upcoming ribbon cutting ceremony for some newly built quarters, right before the next Songkran. The holiday was something like New Year's Day, for the Thai's. All the women in the prison, who participated in the festival, would drench each other with a bucket or cup of water for good luck. It went on for days, and they all seemed to really enjoy the three-day fest.

In 1997, I braided my hair back and let them douse me completely, but only once. American's were joining in on the event, and I had to see what the deal was. It was a different type of vibe, sort of unexplainable, considering the predicament we were all in. The officers weren't as relaxed about the water fest that particular time. The two events were clashing, and they were running around in circles like banshees, mixing us together for appearances sake before different visitors came in, which oftentimes was without much of a warning. They'd been coming in early for viewings, and so many monks were in and out, sometimes with only a few minute's notice, wanting a glimpse at the finished product.

As the ceremony approached, a rather large donation was much talked about. It had been given to the women's section of Klong Prem for the construction project, which was what all the curiosity revolved around. The new building was double the size of the other ones. It looked out of place next to all the surrounding older structures. A few Thai official viewing parties had already come in to see the end results for the news story. They were given photo opportunities. The pressure was put on everyone in the prison. Mainly when the officers wanted to look good and have a favorable impression in the eyes of their superiors. There had been two Chinese girls fighting a couple of days prior in the middle of an important visit, embarrassing the Khuns. It made them extra cranky. They'd started patrolling more frequently.

There was no hiding out or getting lost, so to speak, during that timeframe. Out of nearly one thousand women inside of Lard Yao, maybe eighty of us didn't work. There were about ten Americans, thirty Nigerians, a handful from some of the other countries. A few drug addicted Thai's, who were detoxing, weren't forced to work, even though it was supposed to be mandatory for them. The withdrawal and recovery stages were rather lengthy, so going cold turkey was brutal.

We roamed around with nothing but minutes to burn throughout the work time hours. It wasn't all idle time for each individual, as one group of non-workers had begun taking accredited GED class through the mail system. Another group started a church. All of those activities were put on hold during these particular visits because they required our full attention.

Periodically sitting underneath the biggest tree on the front side of the grounds, afforded me a bird's eye view of all the activities. I didn't need someone to come and find me on important days. It also gave the Khuns the impression I was not being a difficult foreigner and wanted to stay in the loop but assumptions can be tricky.

I wasn't interested, not even a tiny bit, in their latest circus act. Nonetheless, I'd began to be somewhat okay when hanging out in the open spaces of the compound during the day. Nobody bothered me whenever my head was tilted back against one of the shade trees unless it was necessary. After a period of time, the pictures, which would form mentally while isolating myself too much, left me in a trance-like state. Whenever daydreaming about revenge, I felt restless and had become more like a nightmare, even when the sun was shining.

All of a sudden, one stifling, hot day, I'd awoke with a serious determination to pull out of the dark hole, of conscious depravity. It'd become a necessity for me, especially after witnessing cowardly Khun Soon Moe Lee's torture tactics against an inmate in living color. It all started at a certain point to make me feel like something terrible had attempted to take over a portion of my soul. Inexplicably, I'd had two dreams with religious connotations shortly after the run in with the officer.

One was a perfect image of what I perceived to be Christ. Even though no words were spoken, it'd given me a pervading sense of peace. The second dream was more apocalyptic, but no message was technically given, which rocked my world. As much as I'd backslidden in my Christianity, it made absolutely no sense to me as to why I'd started having such vivid dreams. I sealed my lips shut for fear of being labeled a cool person who'd turned into a fanatic. Silence about something I didn't want to deal with was a well-formed habit already. While secrets aren't necessarily easily kept, it's another form of mind control. They can be told or not.

Pushing on to the next thing quickly always made me feel much better. Why my spiritual beliefs were often in a battle with my heart, making me feel conflicted was increasingly sounding off in my head. Faithful but flawed, I'd mainly enjoyed flying dreams, not only the soul stirring ones. Forcing an inner shift in my spirit, under such stressful living conditions, seemed to be asking a bit much.

If you're not strong enough to recognize what's happening, temporary frailties of the mind can send you into an uncontrollable tailspin. After those visions, however, if a thought passed through my mind about any type of vendetta, I would attempt to Jedi mind trick myself into thinking about something totally different.

I certainly didn't have a thirst for vengeance anymore. Those dreams had been one of the reasons for the fading away, of any revengeful feelings. I'd been silently shaken up so much. Considering that those dreams were more vivid and realistic than any of the other I'd ever experienced in life, I took a serious pause to regain a grip on my emotions.

After years of being completely sober behind Lard Yao's walls, my thought process was somewhat changing. After seeing certain imagery in a bunch of cirrus clouds weeks later as a simulacrum, I knew it was probably a pareidolia episode or a coincidence. Regardless if it was another sign or not, I quietly embraced it and started feeling differently about all of my retaliatory views. Therefore, realizing something more powerful than myself had reframed and possibly changed the game for me. I definitely wasn't ready for it.

MONSOON YEARS

Thailand experiences three seasons: hot, cool and rainy. We always had to go out into whatever the elements were regardless, every day seeking shelter. It was extremely hard on everyone trying to cram into any available cool or dry spaces if they had no job. At least the workers were able to stay put in one spot all day. There was no way to completely block out the cold rain coming in from the forceful winds of the monsoon. It was always the absolute worst time of the year, and a dark wall of clouds seemed to never move.

Many extended hours of rain washed out whole days, making the compound nearly impossible to deal with. During one of the heaviest and wettest monsoon seasons I'd experienced thus far, wind driven sheets of rain pelted the windowless buildings for three days in a row. By sunrise of the fourth day, the weather had settled into a steady mix of blowing rain and torrential downpours, causing everyone's mood to sour. After a major in-house problem, I was called upon after day five of the continuous storms because a couple of my fellow Americans wanted me to help rectify an implausible situation.

"I'm sorry." I stood up. "Telling you guys to talk it out is only making things worst. Just take a vote because there's only so much longer they'll wait around for us," I said.

"Let's just go. The majority have already stated they can't make it throughout next month without it." Tangelo said.

"We can figure this out Kim!" I'd already decided how we needed to proceed after listening to all of their opinions but was feeling more than a little bit leery about their abilities to complete the task at hand.

Out of the thirty-two Americans inside of Lard Yao's walls, eleven of them wanted to circumvent almost waist-deep flooded waters to get to our end of the month Embassy room visit so they could sign for their stipend. It was the only day that the Embassy would be coming out unless an emergency happened. They had braved the inclement weather just to keep their scheduled visit.

We were told there was a partial blockage in the drainage system that couldn't be dealt with until after the rains subsided, which made it terrible timing for us. The male officers had already tried to come in and fix it but weren't successful, and the warden didn't give the Embassy a courtesy call to explain our current plight. Some of us were sitting around the top tier steps of our building watching the flooded waters and the crazy Thai's who had to get through to their jobs because it was mandatory. A couple of the girls had fallen into the water on their way to work, and the whole prison was a sloppy mess. The compound was inundated because of the monsoon.

That wasn't the first time that Lard Yao had experienced flooding. Over the past three years I'd been inside so far, the waters had risen up above our ankles on numerous occasions. The other American women weren't interested in getting to the Embassy room visitation area. They had outside sources of income coming in from their family on top of receiving the government's money.

They didn't want or need to try what we were about to attempt. I had enough in my account to make it through also, but there was someone in the group I was close to. With her, my buddy, and my other cohorts all needing to go out there, formulating a plan to get us across wasn't a hard choice to make, in my mind. There was no going around the water as they had hoped. We had to go thru it.

After everyone seemed to understand what I'd opined, there was nothing left to do but get to it. I took a deep breath and said, "Alright, everybody lock arms with the next person. Get ready to hold on tight once you come off that last step." It was going to put a huge spotlight on top of us, as the other inmates watched what we were about to do. Anything the Americans did always seemed to receive lots of attention, whether good or bad.

It had been such a surreal day. Regardless of how many things I'd experienced in life, I always know that my memory bank is still being filled. The visual of watching the girls as they stepped into that water holding hands, first to get their bearings and courage up, as we formed groups of six was captured inside of me forever. I knew they were scared but determined. Honestly, I never had a whiff of fear about doing it, as much as I just didn't want to tread thru that muck. Once I'd gotten further out into the water, a twinge of nerves crept up and a lump was in my throat because the current was pushing us extremely hard.

It was still pouring down buckets of rain. After every plodding step we took, the questions were coming at me like we were on a road trip.

"Are we walking on the sidewalk? "What's that floating towards us!?" "Do you think the Embassy is still out there waiting?" A plethora of other questions were directed towards me.

It was at that point that I had a major regret. I'd told one of my cohorts about some of the tough situations from my days in basic training and how much I'd endured to become a squad leader after week one. Both of my drill sergeants had acknowledged my daily efforts. They'd always made it a point in the first few days of training to reference me and the only other person from my state as country, strong girls. It didn't take too long before I'd earned their merit. Then they only referenced me by my last name.

Those tales from days gone by had been cathartic for me and amusing to her. However, guiding everyone through the storm and saying that it would be easy was inaccurate. The problem frightening everyone was the heavy amount of debris, which was in the water. It was definitely creepy to the other girls. Luckily, the droplets of rain had begun to dissipate before we'd entered the Embassy Room visiting section.

They were allowed inside of a conference room to visit with the Americans, but we sat on the outside talking to them thru a small open portal. It made visits more personable but still secure enough for the consular. After we'd made it thru and back in, the girls weren't all linked up anymore. Everybody had gone sloshing back with their friends. My group quickly became smaller with only Tangelo and my other confidant, Irene, walking by my side. No one was afraid anymore, but that's how I preferred it. I desired to help everybody else if I could, whenever needed, and then stay out of their way. The rest of the evening everyone was somewhere telling a different version of their time spent walking thru the flooded prison. I tried to be as engaging like the others, but it was difficult. Two days later, the sewage system was fixed, and things were routine again.

A week after the major flood, an unpleasant picture wouldn't stop popping into my thoughts. I hadn't been completely forthright with one of the ladies. She had asked me a specific question while walking thru the swirling debris. The whole episode still bothered me, mainly because it'd become a constant topic of discussion on the compound for days afterwards. So many of the rambling questions asked while in the midst of our walk seemed like nervous energy from a couple of them.

When one girl asked about a black object floating in the water toward us, I'd said something as to not panic her. Since her voice was high pitched already, I told her to keep going because it was only a log. However, it wasn't a log; it was a snake moving uncontrollable in the swift current. I'd looked straight into his beady eyes but luckily the vortex moved him away merely seconds before the freak-outs would have begun.

At age of eighteen, as a young recruit, I once had an encounter with a snake den around the woodlands of Fort Jackson. I definitely wasn't up for another confrontation like that. On a rare, two-day weekend pass, during the mid-eighties, I'd stayed on post instead of going home. There'd been a lot of talk from the drill sergeants about the overpopulation of wild hogs. They were surrounding Suicide Hill, the location our weekday runs. Wanting to do some hunting on my down time and party with some new friends, I kept hanging around. No one else, who'd stayed on base, had felt like doing any early morning tracking during their off time, so I'd ventured out alone. After a lengthy, unsuccessful feral hog hunt, I happened to slide over the edge of a sandy soil pit filled with curled up snakes. My attention had been diverted by a bird's nest. Walking while looking up had turned out to be a bad combination. My binoculars flew off, but thankfully the sling on my Marlin guide stayed attached. I didn't slip all the way down to the bottom, but it was close enough.

When I looked over my shoulder, while digging my fingers and boots into the dirt to climb out, I realized they hadn't really budged. Just a couple of them seemed to have stirred. The adrenaline rush and nervous energy took me over the top pretty fast. After getting out of the hole and running a few steps, I started almost immediately descending the slope of the hill, and my momentum was too much.

It'd catapulted me so quickly down the incline. I was in serious jeopardy of plummeting over if I didn't slow down. I reacted by grabbing at some vines in order to help me break the pace. The idea worked, but not without its consequences. I immediately realized there were some welts and cuts on my hands.

There was warm blood, rolling down the right-side of my cheek. I was rushing back to the barracks. It didn't hurt when I wiped at it, so there wasn't a panicked feeling, but my heart was still racing. Once I was able to assess my injuries in a mirror, it was worse than imagined. Some of the stems from the tree branches, I'd dashed past, had cut me in the face twice like a blade.

I didn't go and seek out medical attention to get stitched up. An explanation would've been warranted because of not having a South Carolina hunting permit. They would've also wanted to know how I had access to my own personal rifle and if my vehicle was on post, all of which was forbidden for trainees.

I'd put two small bandages on my face and continued my weekend instead. At the same time, speculation soon ran rampant in my unit. They were talking about some of the things that could've happened to me. The nosey soldiers came up with their own conclusions because there was nothing for me to tell them. However, I did learn not to venture out into the woods without a companion nearby.

After a whole lot of pondering, one thing was for certain. I hadn't thought about the cause of the small scars on my face in over ten years. That was until the flooding catastrophe happened. I would've felt beyond terrible if one of the ladies had fallen into the filthy water or had been hurt by anything floating, since I'd reassured them we'd be fine.

As much as being incarcerated had cracked open my inner vision, it had also become one of my greatest sources of pain. It wasn't only physically dealing with the elements. Sometimes it hurt mentally, being locked away inside of Klong Prem. That day of wading in an engorged, cesspool of water had become unforgettable to me. I'd decided to never discuss that snake with anyone behind the walls of Lard Yao.

In early 1998, constant rumblings about the financial crises surrounding the country of Thailand started spreading throughout the entire compound like a wildfire. The economic collapse and political unrest had caused the devaluation of the Thai baht. It was the precursor for almost weekly updates from the Khuns about distraught businessmen jumping off the roofs of their high-rise office buildings. Some of them just couldn't accept going bankrupt. It was the main topic of conversation for months on end because the visits the Thai inmates randomly received had become more scarce the past few months. They were feeling the stinging, residual effects of the calamity and were in a panic worrying about their loved ones.

Normally, the chaotic climate would've affected all of us but not that time. About five months prior, one of the first set of Americans ever to transfer back into the United States from Lard Yao had taken place. Some of them had been incarcerated a couple of years past their eligibility due date. Now that the treaty was formally in place, they'd been the first priority. My group's transfer, however, was on schedule. The approved arraignments had been made already, which consisted of about seven of us.

The way some of the ladies were walking around, I was sure the buildings could have burned down to the ground, and we still would've been okay. Even if we'd had to sleep out on the grass during the waiting period, our attitudes were of nervous anticipation. Knowing the end of the tumultuous ordeal was coming soon, we were eagerly waiting on the Embassy for our official itinerary.

A much talked about inside visitation from a couple of local news reporters came around during the same time as the majority of Thai inmates were becoming increasingly aggravated. The media personnel wanted to report on the children's nursery, which had been recently renovated. No filming was allowed on the premises. Isolated instances allotted for that kind of picture taking, according to the prison officials. Donated monies were always on display. Any type of construction or repairs at Lard Yao made headlines. So many times over the years, we'd often been told by the Embassy how the men never received donations to ease their cramped living conditions.

Honestly, the information didn't make us feel any better. What we, the women, were enduring monthly was like being in hell on earth. Nobody on our side of the walls really had much energy leftover to sympathize too much with them. The majority of the inmates were in no mood for the latest grandstanding by the officers while the bahts on their books were steadily dwindling. The Thai government had never given them any supplemental money no matter how dire their situations were. Some of the Khuns had been working longer shifts too, which was noticeably making some of them crankier than usual. In the aftermath of our brief run in a few months prior, I'd tried to stay away from Khun Soon Moe Lee, who was an officious, mean-spirited woman.

On the day the reporters came in, security was airtight. They didn't want any of the foreigners talking to the press at all. She was unfortunately the officer in charge of watching over all of the non-workers, who were all crammed into the Gongolian. The whole time she was in the building, her frequent glare towards me was so obvious. It was like she was trying to bore a hole through me, and I found that to be such a humorous but immature thing. She knew the extent of what her actions could ever be against me. Realizing staring back at her would've been a wasted effort; I decided to do what was best for me.

I'd started talking about old soldier escapades to the females sitting around my bench. Nothing happening around me seemed to matter too much. I was going to stay safe and out of trouble for the next several months. The warden allowed us to send out a few items to the missionaries. In turn, they would mail home some of our personal belongings to our families. My letters and pictures were my main concerns. I also had been keeping a couple of coins I'd found by a tree in the back of the prison. One appeared to have the Kings face on it, so I figured it may have some value to it.

I was almost out of that hellhole. Khun Soon Moe Lee hated working in that low paying job, according to her, and would probably never change occupations. Her misery was sketched on her face. Surely my constant grin was prickling the Khun, but I didn't care. My thoughts were only about how much longer it might take before my feet were firmly planted back on North American soil.

A memory for me to forever behold came around during the latter part of 1998. That's when I eventually received my coveted transfer papers from Thailand. My departure from the jungle couldn't have come at a better time. The prison was incorporating various changes in order to get a stronger grip on the inmates. They'd started building small fences to keep everyone off the grass, and away from the trees. The next measures to be implemented were going to be setting up surveillance cameras and monitoring equipment. The compound was already eighty percent in their control, but it wasn't enough for them.

In my small group, we were given a couple of hours in which to pack up and get ready to leave. Since it was only the second major transfer between the two countries, there were a lot of extra security measures being taken. They didn't even give us a day's notice. It wasn't the packing that wound-up being time-consuming but the saying of personal good-byes. That ironically was the most difficult and lengthy part of it all, even though it was time to simply focus on myself. There were still well over twenty Americans that were being left behind.

It was hard to leave the women from some of the other countries in such a detestable place. There would be no more outdoor communal showers or squatting over a hole in order to take a crap. I'd persevered throughout all of the madness of Lard Yao, and now I was being released from its grasp. When walking out of those doors for the last time, as everyone was waving goodbye to us, I returned the gesture, but my mind was already busy compartmentalizing away from that wretched place.

Once we'd left Lard Yao and were away from the confines of Klong Prem, the Thai officers rushed us to the airport. Then we were remanded over to a couple of United States Air Marshals. They led us to a small back room in the airport and started manacling us down like we were vicious fugitives. First, we were handcuffed, and our ankles were also shackled. Afterwards they took us out to be boarded and seated first in the back of a plane before the other passengers arrived, since it was an International flight.

It was a most uncomfortable situation even though we weren't chained to each other. Being individually restrained to the limit, however, felt like they had hogtied us. Some of the ladies voiced apprehension while a couple of the others were relaxed with broad smiles across their faces. I, on the other hand, was stoic about it all. The officers let us speak freely amongst ourselves on the long flight. When the meals were served, we all managed to eat while handcuffed, which was humorous and sad at the same time.

After several hours of shifting around, I closed my eyes but not to drift off to sleep. My granddad had passed away a few years back, shortly after I'd been incarcerated. The grievous feeling about missing his funeral had never assuaged. He was a Navy Veteran. Our family patriarch had been a strong willed, self-taught businessman. Becoming one of the first men of color to own two laundromats in my hometown was a major feat.

That man was venerated by the community for his generosity toward the less fortunate. He'd taught me how to run a laundromat, drive, hunt, and fish. After starting the eleventh grade, he bought me a brand new, red 1985 Ford Escort GT Turbo with a sunroof and tinted windows. When I totaled that car a few months later, flipping into a ditch, he got me another ride the next day. It was a white 1976 Ford Pinto, and it looked like a plastic bowl. It was a major step down, but the punishment was understood. It had been my own fault for showboating, but we were both amazed I wasn't physically injured in the accident. I was wearing my seatbelt.

Thinking back to all the things my grandfather had done for me in my youth was needed at the moment. The good times we'd once shared on occasions while crabbing with our homemade nylon pot put a smile in my heart. Those were much better thoughts than the alternative. I didn't want to wrap my head around the reality of what was truly concerning me. An Asian pilot was actually flying me across shark infested waters while I was constrained inside the bowels of a jumbo airliner.

FED-CON AIR EXPRESS

Perhaps, over a period of time, I'd surmised that day would've been a more joyous occasion. After a lengthy flight, we arrived safely in California without incident. Immediately after we disembarked, the demeanor of the U.S. Marshals in charge went from calm to a more serious tone. There was to be no talking whatsoever. The wave of heat was so intense it felt like the asphalt melting, and we were stepping into a haze of steam.

Shuffling across the hot tarmac while in a single file line, almost everyone I'd passed by resembled some sort of caricature. A group of male inmates were fettered and walking directly across from us in the opposite direction. They'd unloaded from a panel van and were being led to a nondescript plane. Some of them were being taken to different court appearances while others were going to jail or penal institutions.

There were several guards armed with shotguns lined up along the airfield between the tail of the plane and transportation vans. Then we were loaded up and whisked away. As the city sites went by in a blur, I glanced out of the window to soak it all in. We arrived at the downtown detention center and were slowly processed in. That was the first of many upcoming strip-searches I would be subjected to.

After all of the booking and intake paperwork was completed, we were unshackled and escorted on an elevator. It was eerily silent on the way up to the only female floor of the massive, high-tech building. Once I walked through those doors, my whole perspective changed. How I'd imagined the day would probably end wound up being surprisingly different.

Cautiously stepping into the women's unit, the world automatically snapped back together again. After so many years of constant anguish, while being held overseas, it was a real sense of normalcy. The Metropolitan Detention Center of Los Angeles, California is only used for housing federal detainees. It had an atmosphere similar to that of a decent apartment complex.

Only one officer controlled the floor, and they weren't visible or intrusive. We were told the majority of ladies being held were for white-collar crimes. Only a few were note passing bank robbers. There were no so-called dangerous convicts. Everybody that'd transferred from Thailand were assumed to only be incarcerated because of narcotics. Across the waters, and now being at home, I'd never let on to anyone about my other case. Being labeled a drug dealer had suited me fine. In Thailand, whenever an inmate would come in for something violent, everyone treated them differently out of fear.

They had a basketball court out on a huge, outdoor balcony, which had an atrium cover. The separate section for television viewing had ample spacing with a couple of chairs surrounding it, and telephones with no time restrictions. A couple of pool tables and several microwaves were in the common areas, but there was a cold steel feeling everywhere I walked, even though no bars were in sight.

There was an upper floor, but the cells weren't at full capacity, so I was assigned a room downstairs without anyone else in it. A nice wooden desk with a chair, a locker, and a toilet were inside. The mattress was a cheap, plastic one, but it was relatively new. They also had a vent near the top of the ceiling, which some of the ladies used to talk thru to the men in the floor above us whenever they could.

The women accommodated the new arrivals as best they could with hygiene products. After I'd received my bed roll and tossed it on the bunk, the next move I made was calling my mother. Then I had a hot shower and some food. After making several more phone calls to close family members, and since it was late evening, there wasn't time for anything else but lockdown. I'd been on a non-stop flight for over fourteen hours. I hadn't even sat down once since being in the facility.

Strangely, instead of being tired, I felt invigorated. After the guard locked the already closed beige, steel door with the small glass window across it, my thoughts began racing. I put a pillow down on the floor, which was a great feeling to have the luxury of deciding what I wanted to do in private, before lights out without anyone gawking. Kneeling down and quietly praying was all I could do. A loud thank-you, Lord, and praising him the way I really wanted to would've made me seem like a loon to some of the others. Therefore, I kept it silent and stretched out on a bed for the first time in over four years. It felt awesome. No annoying background noise from a Thai television made the night even more tolerable.

The complete solitude was welcomed. There was no struggle to get comfortable, which was in stark contrast to life in Asia. Not having to draw from the more pleasant side of my memories, for a little bit of easement, was wonderful. After an extremely long day, my nerves needed rest. Knowing the lower limb of the golden sun had already darkened into a fiery red, I started relaxing my racing thoughts. The central air was something wonderful I hadn't felt in years, and it was definitely going full blast in the building. It was working too perfectly. I was shivering but humbled. Eventually, I fell off to sleep, feeling ever so grateful to be back in The U.S. Having access to normal amenities wouldn't erase one fact though. Regardless of where I was, it was horrendous being caged up anywhere.

On the second day of being inside of the detention center, the feeling of being completely in tuned with everything around me was a bit weird. There was plenty of continuous inmate movement. Basically, there were minimal rules other than a zero-tolerance policy for stealing, and no fighting was allowed. We were free to do whatever else within reason, inside of the boundaries. I walked around the small basketball court out on the balcony most of the day. A week later we had surprise room inspections. It was a big spectacle. The corrections officers only found unauthorized food items in some of the lockers. They appeared pleased to be able to justify their actions.

Around the twentieth day, sitting back and watching television was my only activity other than using the phone. I did take the time to notice a set of the Americans that'd came with me from Thailand were being transferred out every couple of days. There'd been seven of us, and the officers had already said we would be a priority to be sent to our next stop.

A classification had been made of the first group, who'd arrived a few months prior to us. Some were determined to be suffering from post-traumatic stress disorder symptoms. They wanted each one of us sent to prison or camp and processed out as soon as it was legally possible. After a couple of weeks had passed by, everyone else that had been in my group was gone. None of the officers said anything to me about it. I didn't ask any questions either because we all knew when it was our time to leave, we would definitely be called.

There were women trying hard to get my attention in a variety of ways. Usually I blew them off with a smile because of the circumstances. I wasn't quite ready for any friendly chatter. I'd realized quickly that an old, unresolved case was upon me sooner than I thought it would be. There was a feeling of nervous energy building up inside of me about the dreaded ordeal. I'd been preparing for a long time to deal with it.

Right after noon chow, during the second month, a young woman, Brenda, walked up to me while I was shooting pool. She challenged me to a match. After knocking a few balls in, she asked me an odd question, which temporarily took me away from the trappings of my consciousness. It also led me directly into the path of one totally interesting woman.

"Do you know how to play bridge, Kim?" While holding a cue stick in one hand, Brenda was looking from the corner of her eye over at me instead of the pool table.

"Yes, actually I do. Why, what's up?" I murmured. She started telling me about a group of Caucasian women, who sat at a table everyday playing a card game. One of the white girls had previously made a bet with her roommate that they'd never find a black or Hispanic inmate who would even try to. The rumor mill was no women of color had the patience or conceptual capabilities to play it.

If someone did before she left, the reward would be them receiving free commissary for six months once they got to prison. If they didn't find somebody, the loser would perform a few chores. There were only five people in the building who knew how to play. I was given some personal information pertaining to what was known about them because that's what most women do when they're locked up. There were always the gossipy busybodies, who cared too much about other people's cases. In that instance, I was glad she'd briefed me about that clique of women's criminal past. One of them was a boss in every sense of the word.

I was more knowledgeable than most, about the intricacies involving the particular card game. I'd been in a bridge club before and was an excellent bidder. After all the introductions were made, they quickly put me to the test. The girl that they'd paired me up with was initially quite chilly. During the course of the first game, she made a biting comment, stating she'd been taught blacks were a sub-division of the human race.

Initially, I was more appalled than angered, but I didn't let any emotion be shown. Telling her bits and pieces about my upbringing and previous career choices seemed to enlighten her. I'd left out any worthless, ignominious details, which could be scrutinized. Anyway, when all was said and done, having a lofty manner had landed both of us in the same rocky boat.

After we'd won three games in a row, the reception warmed up. The next day, after breakfast, I immediately went back over to their table but was partnered up with a different woman, who was obviously controlling the bunch.

For several reasons, playing bridge is a long, drawn out game. There's not a lot of talking usually because of the concentration level needed. My new partner seemed very inquisitive since she'd been told I was one of the Thailand transferees. With her opening up the sporadic banter almost immediately, it gave me a lane to jump into and ask a few questions about her incarceration.

Each day, for the next couple of weeks, I looked forward to flipping cards over with those women and didn't feel any lingering tentativeness from anyone of them. It took my thoughts away from why I was still sitting in California, which was something the other available activities hadn't accomplished.

As we were getting into a comfortable groove, the leader of the group was called out to be transferred to FCI Dublin Women's Prison. I didn't even get a chance to say goodbye and doubted that she even cared about any of us. With all of the pressures she was facing emotionally and monetarily, inmates weren't on her list. The day she left was as if the air had been let out of the building by her presence being gone. I'd felt from the start, once she'd been receptive to playing cards and mingling with me on her level, all would end well.

She was a rather wealthy woman, only three years older than me. With such a high-profile case, her influence around certain inmates had been visible. It was something about the way in which she carried herself. As soon as she wanted anything, her minions seemed thankful for the task.

The only Caucasian woman I'd ever met in my entire life, who'd commanded attention in a powerful way, was a staff sergeant. She'd once been over my military units. When I was stationed in Fort Knox, KY from 87' to 89,' she was as tough as nails NCO. That woman earned respect and power, without being unlikeable, just as easily as the civilian madam was doing on the daily.

Unfortunately, with me being out of the country, when her crimes had been nationally televised, that had been my first-time hearing about her many exploits. Both of my siblings had heard about her escapades before. When I informed my sister I'd been playing bridge and talking every day with the famous Hollywood Madam, she was extremely surprised. With only fifteen-minute recorded telephone conversations permitted at a time, there wasn't much conversing to be had. It was just enough light banter to reassure my loved ones I was doing okay.

The next enthralling person who piqued my interest wasn't someone I talked about to my family, ever. Regardless, she would have a brief, yet eye-opening part in my life during the time spent waiting and spinning my heels around in MDC Los Angeles.

On the second month after being back in the states, I'd started to loosen up quite a bit. It was mainly due to the fact of me realizing these ladies had similar backstories as the other women who I'd already done time with in Thailand. Their crimes had just been committed here at home. The staff at the detention center was a lot more compassionate than the Thai guards had ever been.

They were much easier to talk with for obvious reasons, since there were no communication barriers. I rarely shot hoops or played pool. Most days were spent listening to west coast music on my new Walkman or teaching some of the girls how to win at various bridge games. When I wasn't doing that, posting up and watching the entire pod from the top tier, while hanging out and talking with one of the coolest guards around, was my other outlet.

Standing on one leg with his opposite foot perched on the upper balcony's bottom rail was Officer Millerton with his head on a constant swivel. He stood out as a slender, mild-mannered man. Because of his thin body, he wasn't as imposing of a figure like a more muscular man. Eventually after weeks of listening to some of the tales from his former days as a Marine, I knew he was an example of an outward appearance being deceptive. He was a highly decorated veteran, who'd gotten out of the military after thirteen years.

I noted he'd divulged a lot about his time in service but not why he'd been discharged. However, I knew it was honorable, like mine. Otherwise, he definitely wouldn't have been hired on as a corrections officer. He was so chilled out; on his shifts, the inmates barely knew he was around until something was needed.

One day he'd came in and showed me an adult magazine and then pointed out a young woman who was sitting alone in front of the television. She'd been brought in the previous day. Most of the males, on different floors of the building, were already buzzing about her. They were sending notes through the orderlies who'd brought over the food trays. When it was possible, they'd holler through the vents. That was another communication outlet.

I'd seen her first enter the building and thought she was just another new, pretty inmate. There were plenty of those, who were West Coast Natives. After that day I'd introduced myself, and we made an instant connection. Since her name sounded similar to the country I'd just left, I decided to give her a nickname.

Every day we started hanging out together and talking about so many different topics. She talked about the family a lot. The only subject I ever brought up to her was about Thailand, when we weren't busy discussing our newfound kinship. Most people seemed intrigued with the thought of an Alabamian flying across the country to smuggle drugs. Sometimes I'd look into her eyes wanting to tell her the truth, but it was too comical and sad for a twenty-three-year old Californian to digest.

The biggest thing I'd learned from her was how a real thief thinks. She was a bank robber, who was already actively plotting and planning her next dangerous heist. She'd received a short sentence after her trial for that case, which her lawyer had worked out for her role in the robbery. Tee's accomplice, who'd been involved in the crime with her, received the most serious conviction. Without fail, at some point during the day, she would talk about and map out different robbery scenarios. Then she would shred the paper into tiny pieces. It was odd to me, but I went along to get along.

I was nobody's judge to offer up an opinion, even if it was strange. She'd been visibly upset about the separation from her young son and boyfriend. I couldn't really grasp the concept of anyone concocting a dangerous bank heist while behind bars for the same type of crime. I didn't mention to her that I'd known about her much ballyhooed, Black Tails photo shoot. Interestingly enough, she never said anything to me about it.

By the time the third month had rolled around, the feeling in the air was one of misery. The pensive sadness was due in large part to the upcoming holidays. The majority of women incarcerated had children. Their emotions during special occasions mirrored what I'd experienced in Thailand. It was always a less joyous time for all the mothers versus the childless inmates. They were moody as hell and everybody knew why. On a day in which I wish could've been taken back, an incident happened that was terrible. Thanksgiving was less than a week away.

Leaning over the upper level railing, while chatting with one of the female guards, was a typical day. We were looking down at the surrounding activities, and everything was calm in the unit until an argument broke out and carried its way upstairs to the officer.

Everything happened quickly. The two girls, who were in the midst of it all, had a large cluster of folks following them up the steps. They were noisily, egging on the drama. By the time they'd reached both of us, the tensions were already so high the guard couldn't contain them. When she tried to get them to stop arguing, one of the girls got right up in the officer's face and started yelling about something.

I couldn't hear everything she was saying. I was watching intently what was unfolding in front of me. The most vocal and irate one of the pair was actually bumping the guard up against the railing! Now, it was common knowledge the correctional officers had no weapons nor pepper spray on the floors. The only device they had was a bulky, walkie-talkie type of radio.

That was the first major dustup that I'd seen in the detention center. It went from bad to worst quickly. I could see the rage in the girl's eyes. The officer appeared to be a deer looking into some headlights. Then, the unthinkable happened. She started trying to push the guard over the edge, and that's when I intervened.

I jumped in and snatched the girl around her collar. "Man, get your damn hands off her!" I screamed in her face. Then, as quickly as it started, it'd ended at the same rate of speed. I remember that inmate giving me one of the most vicious looks, but she didn't swing. I didn't let her go either. Can't really remember how many minutes had passed, but it felt like an eternity. In the timeframe I'd spent tugging with the woman, the officer had obviously alerted the control center. The surveillance cameras only observed the common areas.

Moments later about four officers rushed in before we knew what'd hit us. One of the first responders knocked me out of the way roughly and onto the floor. A knee was pressing into my back. Another one grabbed the other girl, ripping her off her feet and slamming her to the floor. After a brief discussion with the female guard on duty, they scooped up the inmate who had attacked Officer Bledsoe. They escorted her to solitary confinement. The guards immediately regained control of the unit and started shouting for us to lock down.

After they got us all securely accounted for, I sat down on the bed feeling like fresh cow manure. I felt so damn bad I'd gone against another inmate to save an officer. It was really killing my heart, like I'd violated an unwritten code. I didn't even know the girl. I'd known several things about the guard though.

She was an ex-Army medic, and it was an easy comradery which had come about, even though I was locked up. Since we were both prior military, she'd noticed I was different from some of the other prisoners. It made it easier to talk to her and kick it whenever she was on duty. She was also extremely attractive with smooth, cocoa butter skin, which had obviously helped to blur the situation. Though she was engaged, I'd flirted with her relentlessly. Officer

Bledsoe had found it humorous. It definitely helped me to pass the time when she was on duty.

I realized after that day was over why my life had always spun a certain way. It was because I'd never let anyone harm my family, friends, or anyone else I was cool with. Saving other people's hides, however, was a bad habit which needed breaking. I would find out the officer who I'd protected didn't see it that way. She actually found a way, a few months later, to show me how much my actions were appreciated.

After tossing and turning almost the whole night long, my new roommate, who I'd been bunking with for about three weeks, came down to sit on my bed. She just wanted to give me a hug. It was the girl from the adult magazine, and she told me I'd done the right thing. I wanted to confide in her about how many times I'd already stuck my neck out for other folks and their problems. It had become dangerous and tiresome over the years defending other people, but I didn't say a word. I shut my mouth and accepted her consolations.

Right before the Christmas holidays, the next group out of Klong Prem had arrived. I knew they were coming, but I didn't expect to still be in limbo long enough to see them. There was one person, out of the group named Lauren, who I'd grown close to when we were in Thailand together. She had a small, benign cyst removed from one of her breasts while we were over there. I'd been the only person she'd entrusted to change her bandages. Helping her to recuperate under such foul conditions wasn't easy, but we'd managed to keep away any infections. The medical incident had sealed our bond. The night they'd showed up, it was already well after midnight, but when the next day came in, I put on a performance for the ages.

Soon as the doors opened that morning, I started an argument with my bunkmate. I wanted her out of my room. It was a rather obnoxious shouting match, but to Officer Bledsoe came to my defense. She made Tee get out. I asked her if my associate from Lard Yao could move into my room. She said yes. It was her way of paying me back for what I'd done, saving her from falling.

After the ruckus had settled down, it started right back up again that evening when my old roommate recognized what'd happened. She came to my room and tried to get into a fight with me. I was trying to close the door to keep her out, but she had the better leverage on it. Her foot was jammed in the door to block it from being closed. I didn't want to get loud, causing the guard to come back and intervene. My grasp was not good on the door. She was pushing it and matching my strength. I looked over at my pen and pencil on the desk knowing full well what capabilities they both held. I really didn't want to take it to that magnitude. My new roommate was as quiet as a church mouse. She didn't even attempt to help me hold down the fort. I knew she was wondering about the type of mess I had gotten myself into. When my hands started to slip, I could tell that Tee was ready to pounce and try pummeling me. My mind started clicking, and then I blurted out a location to her. That stopped her dead in her tracks, and she looked like she'd just swallowed a spoonful of castor oil.

It was her grandmother's address. I'd once seen it on an envelope, which she'd given to me one day to add to our outgoing mail collection. I didn't mean any real harm by saying it and certainly wasn't trying to stalk her family, but I had an almost photogenic memory. I normally remembered any and everything that passed by my way. She let that door go and looked at me stunned, knowing full well what I'd meant. Incarcerated women with a particular lifestyle weren't always willing to share it with their families.

I slammed the door shut with such force it made my ears ring. There was no legitimate reason to me as to why the situation had escalated to such a degree. We'd only known each other less than two months, but now it was all over and done with. That night my thoughts were consumed with getting the heck out of MDC LA without catching another unwarranted case.

During the last week of 1998, I was called to be transferred out of the detention center. Initial thinking was that a flight to prison was up next, but they took me on a detour. I was driven to and detained at the Riverside County Jail, California. Once inside, the booking process was long. At least the cops were more forthcoming with information, unlike the staff at MDC LA. They'd told me I would be transferred to federal prison after a hold was lifted. There was a warrant out for my arrest for jumping bond. That confirmed what I'd been thinking since being the last one in my group to leave. It was past time, as far as I was concerned, to deal with those old demons.

The female floor had four-man bunks and several mounted televisions outside of all the cells. We were all dressed in oversized solid colored jumpsuits and slip on shoes. Phones were available to use as much as we wanted to, and a section for eating and playing board games was on the opposite end. I was assigned to the last cell on the row, which had two girls already. We all seemed to hit it off well, and I adjusted easily. To me, anything was possible after over four years of the nightmarish, hellhole that I'd just been transferred from.

The glaring thing about jail is realizing that females, during the day, were always going to be loud. It was boring as hell but not stressful in Riverside. It was like being locked away with nothing to do but chill inside of the concrete confines. I didn't worry about too much because everything was completely out of my hands. I'd only been locked away in county jail less than two weeks before there was a small earthquake. It was an alarming feeling that jolted me out of my sleep. When I woke up one of my cellmates, she told me to relax because it was not that major. The whole building swayed, but she'd told me it was designed to rock that way. It felt like falling from the peak of a rollercoaster. There were no aftershocks, so I got back into my bunk.

I stayed awake the rest of the night waiting for the individual on duty to come and patrol the floor. Not one deputy ever came.

I spent the start of the New Year, praying in that cold jail. Days crept by with no change in my status. My cellmates hadn't moved either. Both were awaiting trials without a date in sight. On a day we were making jokey comments about who could make the best tasting ramen soup casserole, a new inmate arrived and screwed up the whole vibe.

The girl that entered our cell was well over six feet tall and walked in with an apparent attitude. She was instantly complaining about everything. She complained about her lawyer, her feet, back, and neck, and why she couldn't be on the top bunk. One of the ladies was trying to help accommodate her. The other girl and I continued on like she wasn't there. After the lights were turned out, and everyone had settled down, I had an uneasy feeling about that girl. While lying on my bunk reading a book with the dim light, I could hear the new girl muttering to herself. That was never a good sign in prison, especially when we knew it was a weirdo doing something like that.

After a couple of days, things were getting back to what was normal for us in the tiny cell. The latest bunkmate was still exhibiting some unusual quirks outwardly. Whenever she would get off the telephone, she would come back into the cell and start pacing in a small circle. She was cursing about her family like we cared. It was already becoming an irritant, but what could I do? During part of the long booking process, the police had been meticulous in explaining the rules.

The police sergeants rarely walked the floor unless they were dropping off a riffled thru newspaper. That was another place that seemed like we were on our own until it was mealtime. However, it wasn't even close to the misery of doing time in Asia because we weren't outside living like savages. One day, a sheriff brought in several boxes of dominoes for our cellblock. We'd all started playing and discussing our current plights. I didn't know if I was the only one keeping a secret, but I was determined to stay the course with the drug dealer label. When the kooky new inmate, whose name was Heather, sat down on the end of my bunk, the hair on the back of my neck bristled. She asked could she play too, and immediately the oldest cellmate in the room said, yes.

For many of reasons, I didn't want to play with her. I also didn't want to be the first one saying anything harsh to her, so she joined us. We played for a few hours, and everyone seemed to get along fine until we stopped for lights out. When everybody got up to return to their bunks, I noticed a huge red spot on my bed, and one on the back of Heather's prison jumper. Automatically one of the girls started laughing, but I couldn't find the humor in it. I didn't do anything harsh, but I asked the bloody girl, "Hey, can you do something with that blanket?" "I don't want to look at that nasty mess." It was as if I'd said something wrong to her because she turned around and snapped, "No, you get it up country gal."

Time slowed down as I leapt from my bunk and drop kicked her ass. After falling down from the force of the blow and the lack of balance, we started brawling. She pushed me hard into the side of the metal bed, and it felt like my lip was split. I was in lots of pain, which made me angrier. Even though the girl was taller and sinewy in stature, I picked her up and body slammed her. In the ensuing scuffle, somehow her head was banged into the bars and she was knocked unconscious.

When I realized what'd happened, I stepped backwards scared as hell. One of the inmates ran over to the girl on the floor, but she didn't move, and my heart sank. I was halfway expecting one of the cops to come in and clean house, but they were a no-show. The only camera on the floor pointed to the telephones. Since we were rumbling and not yelling, they weren't alerted. It hadn't lasted over a minute. My other cellmate filled some cups with water from the sink and splashed them in the girl's face. That shocked her back into consciousness. Her legs started jerking like she was having a seizure, but they slowly stopped.

Heather was down on the floor for a long time before getting up. She was visibly disoriented. They helped her to get to a bunk, and I just stayed out of the way while quickly stripping down my bed. Even though we didn't get into any trouble, I was still nervous. By the time we'd all settled back down and called it a night, I was still angry. It was directed at my own behavior.

All the praying and challenges I'd gone through hadn't completely fixed my temperament. I could hear Heather whimpering in her bed, which made me feel like a brain-dead moron. On top of that, I had a swollen, sore mouth. There I was sitting in a California lockup with a serious charge still pending in Alabama. I had gotten myself involved in a physical altercation because I'd felt disrespected by a ne'er-do-well, who'd meant nothing to me.

That was the first time during my incarceration that serious thought was given to seeking out a counselor. Attending some sort of stress management classes, I'd been told might be useful at some point during my last stages of imprisonment. They'd offered one-on-one counseling based upon the fact of recently coming from Thailand. I didn't take the offer because the need to control my reactions was something no one else could fix. My constantly taking on of any and all perceived elements of danger or disrespect with violent retaliation wasn't what neither I nor God wanted. I was going to teach myself ways to deal with threats differently or how to avoid them altogether.

I'd made a decision when I was finally flying away from one of the largest continents on earth. I promised myself other people's actions wouldn't dictate my reactions anymore. It'd been less than six months since I'd returned to the states. I was already failing miserably in the turn the other cheek department. There was one thing I'd never forget about the fight with the girl in county jail. After our little dustup, she stopped acting like such a raving lunatic for the remainder of our stay in the tiny, overcrowded cell.

Overdue emotions surfaced in the middle of January 99' when I was finally allowed to be flown to the main transit center in Oklahoma City. Shackled with a black box attached to my handcuffs, leg irons and a belly chain, I was transported via an aircraft. The pilot kept flying into frequent air turbulence. The high winds ripping through made us teeter-totter. It was the same feeling I'd once had aboard a rocky, military cargo plane. The entire trip was excruciating. The carrier was completely filled to the brim with male prisoners and two timid looking females. I noticed the other ladies didn't have their hands secured with any secondary locking mechanisms. I imagined the precaution was meant for the so-called dangerous felons. I'd been told the plane was aptly named Con-Air by the inmates. We were like cows bumping around in an old cattle car, but it was good to be on the move, which wasn't taken for granted.

I didn't even get up to use the bathroom the whole time because of the embarrassment. It seemed the officers were thinking I was a flight risk. That was a terrible misconception. However, if the guards wanted to treat my case like it was different, I understood the rules of their job. It put the wrong type of people in my business, but it was also my shield. I couldn't worry about what anyone else thought because without the box on inmates still would've been talking. Preconceived notions were formulated and whispered about whomever, when no additional info was made available to them. The majority would often gossip about other inmates for sport.

After double digit hours of flying, we arrived in Oklahoma and were escorted into an intake facility. It was around the size of a football stadium. We walked down a long corridor to a platform. Each inmate was on an embarrassing display as we had our shackles removed. Most of the day was spent in and out of process stations, which made for a hard day mentally and physically. They had a little metal toolbox in one room labeled Shakedown Kit. The health checkup took the longest. They checked us out similar to a dissection.

Afterwards, the officer doing all of my escorting put me into a huge holding tank with three wooden benches. There was no place for any stretching out because it was already filled almost to capacity. Waiting for my name to be called and assigned to a room took hours after the in processing.

After the dorm assignment, it was once again a feeling of being completely on my own. There were cameras in the common areas only. The officer's main concerns were only about prisoner movement at chowtime and accountability at lockdown. They never let us outside, and it was like being in a haunted house with a lot of strange men staring at us, looking listless and zombielike.

There were televisions and a spot for the smokers. I mainly stayed on the phone or in my two-man room. I was freezing in that building and bored but so was everyone else, I'd supposed. My cellmate was from FCI Danbury Prison and was being transferred because of a fight that she'd been involved in. She gave me the lowdown on all the details about the FEDS and how anyone caught violating the smallest of rules were immediately sent into solitary confinement, then written up to be eventually relocated and pegged as a troublemaker.

Since we were in the same room, we basically stuck together. Jasmine was similar to the other women I'd already done time with. They liked to talk a lot and speak on the gory details of their pasts, whether it was about what had landed them in prison, or deeply personal revelations about their lives. I was a good listener. Whenever I did decide to have a conversation, it was about Thailand.

Absolutely everything else was off limits and not up for discussion with a convict who was unfamiliar. I'd accepted and realized a few years into my stint in Lard Yao that we were all on the same level, collectively locked away. Thankfully, I was never desperate enough for anyone to hear out of my own mouth about the missteps that'd landed me behind bars. Most of the women always seemed to need at least one earpiece. I heard so many sad tales; over the years they were starting to all sound the same.

Instead of heaping my unbelievable set of tragic events onto their laps, just listening to and encouraging certain inmates made me feel useful. I didn't even tell the missionary I'd grown close to in Asia about everything that happened in my cases. He would've been sadder than he already was about my misfortune. Four days into my detainment in Oklahoma, I picked up a piece of paper, which was placed on my pillow. After reading the note, the mood in the room was changed because of its stupid contents. It was a letter written by my new cellmate, who was professing her desires for me. She'd asked me boldly if I would be her girlfriend.

I was appalled and outdone that she would dare write me such foolishness when she didn't even know me. Just because I'd been kind and listened to her, it had been taken the wrong way. I was offended that she would think I could see her in such a way. She looked like a steroid injected, chocolate giant from the land of misfits. Immediately, I went looking for Jasmine. Finding her hanging out in the exercise area, I told her to meet me in the room. Without hesitation, I put the kibosh on her feelings towards me. That wasn't something even in the realm of my thoughts at that point. Any silly little crushes would have to take a backseat. The girl was so upset by being rejected; it made her openly cry. I refused to console her and decided to lie down on my bunk. Undoubtedly, the situation had become awkward.

After seven days of waiting on the paperwork for sending me to the institution closest to my home state, I was finally designated a prison. The desperation of getting out of Oklahoma was threefold. It was a few days before my 31st birthday, which was coming up on Groundhog Day. I definitely didn't want to spend the occasion in a room with my nutty cellmate.

They flew me back out on Con-Air, another horrific ordeal. I ate the lunch they'd passed out with some assistance from the female sitting next to me. I was still quite embarrassed about the black box attachment on my wrist restraints. I held my urine the whole flight.

The hobbling was just another obstacle. It would be dealt with and pushed away like all the rest of the ugly memories, which I'd learned to block out. Nonetheless, I was making real progress towards the next hurdle of getting back to the South. I was ready to deal with the past and get a relentless monkey off my back. That's all that truly mattered to me. The fact that I'd be able to watch my beloved Atlanta Falcons play in the Super Bowl made getting the heck out of Oklahoma even better.

Processing was relatively quick when I arrived at FCI Tallahassee in Florida. Once the guards assigned me to a unit and escorted me into the main section of the prison, it was like walking onto a college campus. It'd already been described to me by several inmates over the last few months. Seeing it on my own had quickly changed that visualization. There was no gun tower but a fence too tall to scale surrounding the outskirts of the prison. Those security measures were an afterthought once we were inside the gates. No one would be trying to escape.

I'd been on several campus grounds during my young adult years when attending certain sporting events. Right before I'd been incarcerated in Thailand, I was even able to visit my little sister's dorm room in Huntsville. It was for a family tour during her freshman year of college. That federal institution mirrored that type of setting.

There were four large buildings setup as units with no surveillance cameras inside. Only the main building and the hospital were monitored. They had an athletic field for volleyball or soccer, a basketball court and a building set aside for table games. They had several paddleball and pool tables. Almost every evening there was a flag football or softball game. The grassy areas were well manicured with park benches spread throughout the compound. A track with surrounding metal bleachers for the spectators was constantly filled up with hundreds of inmates every evening. The yoga people had their own section as did the inmates who preferred aerobics. If we wanted to lie out on a blanket in the grass and smoke a cigar, there was a blind eye given, as long as we were on time for count.

The compound was mostly run by prisoner labor. The staff did a good job of keeping scheduled activities flowing when time permitted. If it wasn't a talent show, there was a dancing competition going on. The next weekend might have been a billiard's or a canasta tournament. There was a large group that gathered biweekly for the Trivial Pursuit and Jenga matches. They had a large selection of games like Monopoly, Scrabble, Checkers, Connect Four, and Chess. I didn't get around to the basic games.

There was no excuse for anyone to be bored in such a place, but a few were. A couple of the women would sit on their beds all day long doing puzzle books. When I would go inside for something, during the work time hours, there were women lying around watching television. There was a suicide prevention team on the premises; they kept a vigilant watch. I didn't understand that type of behavior. It wasn't my problem to worry with though, but they did seem emotionally checked out.

The only woman I'd met since being there, who had a right to be depressed, was a sixty-seven year old woman. She'd taken a drug conviction wrap to save her daughter. Everyone felt bad for the old lady, but she garnered respect, and nobody bothered her. Anyone else moping was inexcusable. The holidays were understandable, but any other time spent being openly depressed was unnecessary. Enough was going on to keep our mind away from the darkness. Overall, there were more women being productive than not.

I'd joined the softball league two weeks after arriving, but my passion had always been basketball. Having turned down a scholarship to attend a junior college bothered me for years. Before my high school graduation in 1986, my mother pleaded with me to take the opportunity to further my education for free. I didn't listen. I'd wanted to be like my father's side of the family, and keep the military tradition going.

I never did play my favorite sport with the other inmates and show off my ball skills. Those girls were out for blood on the court. I didn't need to be accidentally sent off into a rage because of an inadvertent elbow.

There were four large buildings setup as units. The living quarters had bathrooms on one side and the showers on the opposite side. I was just glad there were shower curtains and purchasable shower shoes. They also had an honors dorm on the far end of the prison, which we weren't supposed to go into. When I walked inside of it briefly to meet up with someone I'd known from Kentucky, it appeared as if they were living in an apartment complex.

I didn't tarry around in there long and only went inside their building a total of three times. They didn't even eat with us, and they rarely came out on the compound. That was understandable. Their living situation was as close to home as it could get so there was no real need to. The punishment was swift for those risk-taking inmates, who sometimes made their way past security to visit the special inmates.

A hospital with a nurse's station was also on the compound, and a small section of each building had a laundry room. When I found out there was a huge law library, I felt that was an added bonus. They had dozens of old, bulky computers. Email service was available, but it was in the inception stages, so no one was really into anything other than envelopes and stamps. There was a chapel and a section set aside for classrooms. There were many inmates who took the full advantage of advancing their educational levels. The prison had a few strict rules they enforced without fail. Absolutely no fighting was on the top of the list, secondly accountability.

The lights came on around 5:30 a.m., so we could get prepared to go eat breakfast if we wanted. Before 9:30, they performed the first count of the day. We had to be sitting in the cubicle or standing by our own partition. It was a major violation if we were absent, even if it was restroom related. Luckily, I didn't have to share my bunk bed with anyone else. I utilized both lockers inside because I was going commissary crazy with all of the choices available.

With over a two-hundred-dollar limit allotted each month, it was going from being underneath a tree to an unlimited array of American food items, and the proper shelter all at once. Some of the women cooked their own food in the microwave. It tasted better than the chow hall. I'd never eaten a mackerel pie or enchiladas lasagna made with diced tomatoes, Doritos, canned chicken and shredded cheese swiped from the kitchen. Each was decent considering the makeshift recipes. They made cakes out of a few crushed bags of cookies and one pint of ice cream. The mix was whipped up into a thin batter. It was cooked up moist and out of the microwave in less than eight minutes. Haagen-Dazs was on the list of commissary items we could buy, and the inmates used their imaginations well. The food in the cafeteria wasn't bad either. There were no cells or bars to be seen anywhere, so the atmosphere in the prison was completely manageable.

It was an open dorm layout with several mounted televisions with a requested daily list on a clipboard of what shows would be viewed on each one. One thirty-inch television was in a sound proof darkened room. Microwaves and telephones were plentiful. When the afternoon rolled around, we prepared for yet another count. There was a longer lapse of time between the evening count and late-night lockdown, which gave the inmates precious moments without being bothered.

Oftentimes after midnight, I could hear the guard on duty walking around doing another check. We were supposed to be sleeping, so most of the late-night owls faked it when they shined the flashlight on our bunks. That was the last time, within a twenty-four-hour timespan, that they tallied up the number of inmates within the units. The next day we would repeat the same cycle again like clockwork.

Unlike every other facility I'd been held in, that one was figuratively a piece of cake. Regardless of the numerous amounts of headcounts, it was more than bearable. The daytime attire was a collared, buttoned up shirt, beige khakis, and a white t-shirt underneath. Whatever sneakers we could afford was okay, and there were a lot of expensive shoes hitting the compound. At night the sleepwear didn't have any type of uniformity, so the girls were all over the place clothes wise. I chose to wear jogging pants and a cutoff shirt.

After a couple of months inside of FCI Tallahassee, I'd blended into my new surroundings. Actively, I stayed working on my pending case in the law library and meeting new people who were doing the same thing. Everything was going so well. I even voluntarily signed up in the kitchen as a hot and cold beverage worker for food service. It was the right thing to do while passing the time away, fitting in instead of being reserved. I also didn't need any empty time on my hands. A few of the inmates appeared too relaxed. There was no way I could tell my family members how my time was being spent each day. It was extremely painful to still be incarcerated, but I didn't feel like a trapped inmate anymore. We had all the physical freedoms we could ask for, under the circumstances. The officers didn't seem to be bothersome at all. My new prison life was moving along without any difficulties until I accidently stumbled into a predicament. There are certain situations, once they are seen, there's no unseeing them. It shook me out of the trance of thinking doing federal time was going to be a breeze.

There weren't many altercations that had occurred during the first several months of my incarceration at FCI Tallahassee. Whenever they did happen, it was always about the same things, either someone had broken the line for the microwave or they had girlfriend problems. It rarely was about the phones or stealing. As soon as trouble hit the compound, we were all immediately put on lockdown. Sometimes we were stuck for lengthy amounts of time, as the officers took care of the problem. On one occasion, the prison had been at a complete standstill for hours because of multiple fights in one of the units. I'd regretfully gotten stuck at work.

The dining area was huge with four restaurant style hard back chairs at each table. It was an easy job working in the chow hall. I was able to move around with much more freedom than the cooks. The staircase outside of the kitchen led to the upper recreational room. I took it upon myself to go up there and shoot a little pool. It was too boring waiting for movement on the grounds to be restored. The double doors upstairs were closed but not locked, and I went inside to knock some balls around. After a few minutes, I started looking for some chalk but couldn't find any. The storage closet for supplies had everything in it but what I needed. Since I was the only one in the room, I walked over to the rec office to see if any was in there. Surprisingly, when I opened the door a black male guard was in there with two Hispanic inmates in an extremely compromising position. Instead of them stopping, to my amazement, the corrections officer screamed at me, "Close the door, asshole. You're supposed to be on lockdown!"

He didn't expect resistance, and I didn't give him any. I immediately did an about face and started making quick time towards the stairwell. I was so pissed off that the temperature inside of my body was steadily rising. The sheer audacity of the man was astonishing. Being in clear violation of the Bureau of Prison's rules and regulations but mad at me for catching him in his dirty act. He definitely knew who I was.

He'd been the officer on duty when I'd won a Valentine's Day pool tournament in the first month after I'd arrived. We'd spoken briefly that day, but it was only about sports. I'd made it a point to go to the rec room at least four days out of the week. Noticing he'd seemed somewhat dismissive with certain inmates and livelier around others, most of the black inmates stayed out of his way. Some people don't like the skin they're born in, but that's another part of the accepted game. There's no jealousy with a black man liking someone outside of our race. It's their business. However, he was the police, and he looked stupid.

In 1987, when I was assigned to my first duty station at the NCO/Drill Sergeant's School in Fort Knox, Kentucky, we were told to absolutely never fraternize with the trainees. So I knew exactly how government property was supposed to be treated. There were at least four guards in FCI Tallahassee who were weak-minded when it came to the female inmates. Taking advantage of a position of power was definitely a criminal offense. They didn't seem too worried about being exposed for their indiscretions. They didn't fully respect their federal job status whatsoever. With close to nine hundred inmates to oversee, the temptation to exploit dozens of women because of their vulnerable positions was too much for some of the male guards to overcome.

Frankly, I never saw a female corrections officer do one thing wrong. In the grand scheme of it all, they weren't that relevant. The inmates and the men ran the prison. It was already common knowledge. Some of the officers were less than discreet about some of the contraband they were bringing inside of the prison. Makeup, cigars, jewelry, weed, alcohol miniatures and perfume were made readily available. Trading privileges, in lieu of cash, was also rampant. A couple of the male officers were known to put money on certain inmate's books for sexual favors. It was a welcoming cesspool if someone wanted to jump in.

When I got back downstairs, everyone was still anxious for the units to be released. It was past time for them to eat and go. I'd pocketed a deck of cards on my way out of the rec room. While I was playing solitaire, there was a calmness which overcame me. I was at peace. My retaliatory mindset was changing for the better, and that incident had shown my growth.

I'd been ever so grateful to get the hell of Lard Yao. Surviving through that entire waking nightmare, with only a few lumps, had me thinking clearer. He was the recreations officer, and I had to respect that. It was the only reason why the paperweight, which was sitting on his desk, didn't suddenly become lodged into his temple. He wouldn't have had enough time to realize that he was slumped over because he'd disrespected the wrong inmate.

Those were the changes that weren't missed by me, and I was proud of holding my peace. I also didn't tell anyone, other than my play brother in the unit. She was sworn to secrecy and kept her mouth shut during our time locked away together. It was too disgusting and funny to not have shared with Patricia.

Humming to herself, the main officer in charge of the kitchen walked briskly throughout the building. She would come in every morning to do a quick inspection. That was the only time I would actually see her until mealtime. The two subordinate officers on duty were more visible but didn't bother any of us too much. My days consisted of working six hours, and it wasn't a difficult task until the units came in.

It was about seven months into my time at FCI Tallahassee, and I was still waiting to be extradited to Alabama. Meanwhile, I was getting a personal crash course in legalese from an inmate, who was a former attorney. We were at the law library most days after I'd gotten off from work. A couple of hours a day were spent learning the jargon and preparing for my upcoming case. I wanted to be my own representation at trial without seeming arrogant. I was innocent and had a lot to say.

When I had time, participating in structured, fun activities were late day stress reducers on the compound. I hardly called home. My immediate family members had driven down to Florida to visit me during the summer. They'd finally seen for themselves that I was okay. That made it easier for them not to worry if they didn't hear from me for a couple of days. In actuality, I had a full scheduled life going on behind the walls. There was no need to be worried about or longing for the outside world. I had no idea of when my full release date would come, so those thoughts were blocked out.

My circle now included a play mother, whose name was Brenda, and my buddy Pat. The three of us were tight. I'd been going to the chapel every weekend and on special occasions. I was spiritually free, and in a good space mentally, but the women were after me. They couldn't understand why I'd been telling people I wasn't interested in having a girlfriend. It was like a smorgasbord of women, and I wasn't hungry, which was ironic.

The busiest day in the chow hall was when fried chicken was cooked. Everybody knew someone who was smuggling food out for sale, their biggest request for quantities. On one chicken day, the kitchen was being heavily monitored, and the cooks couldn't make any moves. One of the cooks asked me to sneak a bag out to one of her friends. She had gotten permission from a young, talkative guard. He and his daddy were both working alternately in the kitchen, whenever added security was necessary.

I was one of the few inmates who had free range to go in and out of the restricted cooking area. I had to constantly go up and down an old elevator shaft to haul and replenish the ice. Other times, I would change out the soda and carbonation tanks. There was a soft serve machine that had to be maintained also. I didn't even hesitate to oblige the cause, and as soon as I stepped through the kitchen door, I was stopped by one of the female guards. In those few seconds, the ceiling felt like it was crashing down around me. I knew that a crisis of major proportions had come into my life in a flash. I was more shamefaced than nervous for some reason.

The guard had me lift up my apron, and she could see the huge bulge in my waistband. There were greasy paper towels surrounding the food, which was bagged in cellophane. Once she identified what it was, she radioed in a code and held on to my arm lightly. In less than a minute, two officers came and one of them handcuffed me. The prison was immediately put on lockdown. I was then embarrassingly paraded through the main artery of the compound and escorted over to the Special Housing Unit.

They weren't playing any games. I was changed out of my freshly creased, white food worker's uniform and strip searched. They ran a specific type of comb through my hair to check for lice, and then allowed me to take a shower. I was given my bedding, basic hygiene items, and a dingy orange jumpsuit with some flimsy flip-flops. Then I was marched down to an isolation cell. After they secured me inside, they had me to bend down on the floor and put my wrists through a small slit in the door. That was how I was to be un-handcuffed.

The room was about the size of a car's parking space. The cell had a metal bunk bed, a thin mattress, a toilet, and a sink. There was graffiti alongside one half of a cinder block wall. A tiny window had a narrow slit that barely let in the outside light. I hadn't been in there long enough to make up my bed before an orderly had come to the door. She asked me if I wanted some reading material. I took the Bible and three other books. I then got everything setup and settled down on the bed. My emotions were all over the place, but I didn't let on. I could hear a couple of the girls in the other cells yelling at each other because speaking in normal tones wasn't audible.

It had all happened at such a rapid pace, but I didn't fret much. It wasn't even dark outside, but I was exasperated by what had transpired. Somehow, I fell off to sleep. In my heart, I knew that anyone who'd ever done time inside of an Asian prison could withstand any conditions. The worst thing about the first night in confinement was the air conditioner blowing to the max. It was like they were trying to kill the Ebola virus.

On the second day of being in the SHU, I was woken up early to eat morning chow. It was still dark outside, maybe four in the morning, and the food was disgusting. I'd eaten better food in Thailand. Punishment was doled out in every way imaginable, whether guilty of breaking the rules or not. No television, phone privileges, or hot food.

There was a routine like clockwork. A chaplain walked through after breakfast and then a therapist.

Several people took meds, I was told, but I declined. They used the antidepressants like sleeping pills. Luckily, I didn't need those types of extreme measures to rest. Before noontime a guard came to my cell and read me the charges. She asked me what happened, but there was no good explanation. I couldn't rat out the cooks, so the outcome was bleak. I had no idea of what the end result would be, but respect is everything behind prison walls and beyond. No one liked a tattletale.

They took me out to rec for about an hour at some point during the day. All I did was walk around in a circle. Every movement in the stinky walkways was heavily monitored, and they dictated the pace totally. Then I was sent to the shower and locked back down. I was in my claustrophobic cell, for over twenty-two hours a day. It didn't take long to realize being in restrictive housing, on top of already being locked up, was not going to be easy. I felt like a popsicle in a deep freezer.

By the third day, I was antsy. There was to be a disciplinary hearing on my case, but I wouldn't be present. The statement the officer had taken, on the previous day, was to be a part of the file. The patterns of the guards were the same as the prior day. The only difference was an inmate, who'd been in segregation for over eight months, was being taken outside. She was not allowed to be around or see any other inmates during her hourly rec time. The rumors told about her in the hole made her lockdown legendary.

They'd transferred her from another prison after she'd thrown a cup of urine in the warden's face. Once she'd arrived in Florida, they'd decided to keep her locked up indefinitely in the SHU. When I leaned against the door and peeked out of my tiny window to get a glimpse of her, she looked massive. Her face had a scowl on it, and with her wild hair, she looked mean as heck. I'd prided myself on being a tough minded individual. That type of punishment was already getting to me after only a few days. I wondered how she possessed the mental fortitude to be able to do it month after month.

It was kind of spooky in segregated. With almost the full day of being locked down and in complete isolation, that wasn't a place for anybody to be held in. Having something to read was okay, but the small spacing, solitude, and cold temperatures made it uneasy. Then there would be sudden loud outbursts from different women randomly screaming for the guards. Most of the time, they were hollering at each other, and that was getting on my nerves. Cabin fever was taking them for a ride. Heaven forbid if one of them was on their time of the month.

During the afternoon of the fourth day, one of the SHU officers came and got me. She took me up to the receiving area to dress out. I was being released. The kitchen guard, who'd allowed the rules to be broken, was encouraged by the cooks and his father to tell the truth. I was told they'd asked him repeatedly. Surely, he didn't want to taint his reputation, but in his deposition, he was honest. I didn't ask what type of consequences he incurred. I knew it wasn't too bad because he was still on the compound.

The sun was a newfound friend when I stepped out of the SHU. I was so damn happy to be out of that dungeon. Walking fast down the main section of the compound, I started swinging my arms to and fro. There was true elation after being sprung from that mousetrap. It felt marvelous. The first thing I did was get on the phone and then take a long, hot shower. Instead of breaking out some of the commissary in my locker, I decided to go to the chow hall and eat their food.

First, making sure my hair, jogging suit, and Nike's were on point. As soon as I went through the chow line, the head officer in charge pulled me aside. She asked if I wanted my job back. That was exactly what I'd anticipated happening. She knew I'd been a trustworthy worker. I was more than happy to tell her, "Hell no." Then I sat down within her eyesight and leisurely ate a cheeseburger with fries. I drank a soda and had a bowl of ice-cream. It wasn't her fault her coworkers were posers, but she didn't vouch for me when she'd heard about the truth. One of the guards from the SHU had passed along the tidbit of information on my way out of the door. They liked to gossip as much as the inmates did.

I wasn't working for the time being. Taking full advantage of the extra time off appealed to me, so that I could do some other things. It'd become tiring loading and lugging around carts of ice. I also didn't have to work if I chose not to. There were health restrictions in my file from Asia because of a pituitary gland problem and stomach ulcers. The FEDS also felt like the transferees from Thailand probably had underlying mental health issues after being incarcerated over there under those extreme conditions. That was true for some. However, we'd all managed to make it back to America in one piece.

The next couple of weeks were spent doing whatever I wanted to do on the compound. It wasn't hard to stay out of trouble with so many different things on my daily agenda. It gave me a better opportunity to sometimes work on my case and mingle with the inmates more. A few had been trying to hang out around my little circle, but I'd been blocking it. Now I was experiencing so much free time; I'd started paying more attention to some of the women on the compound. That decision created yet another unexpected disaster.

I wasn't going to the chapel anymore because I didn't want to be a phony person. It happened about a month after I'd stopped working. I'd been using convenient opportunities to pass the time away; I would flirt with a couple of the inmates. I knew a shift was going on with my level of focus. I was spending the majority of the days messing around instead of in the law library.

One day, there were three girls standing around my cube after dinner, and we were hamming it up. That carried on until the late evening count. After the count was cleared, I put on my headphones and kicked back in a chair with my feet on the desk. In a matter of moments, a female from another unit flew into my cubicle area. Before I could even say anything, she took my small, plastic pitcher of ice water and dumped the contents on my head! Then she dropped the container. I was in shock at such brazenness.

She ran out of the unit with me looking at her in utter disbelief. I didn't chase behind her and retaliate. I knew why she'd done it. The lights were still on even though it was getting late. As I started slipping and sliding towards the bathroom area to dry off and change clothes, several inmates were peering out of their cubes. Others were downright staring at me. I walked past them humiliated and drenched. My willingness to simply brush off the situation didn't help.

Quickly, I regrouped and started drying the water off the floor with some towels. One of the ladies had brought several over to me, and they were desperately needed. I got everything back situated and sat down on my bunk to breathe. Maybe ten minutes after that, several officers came storming into the building. One of them checked my inmate badge and then handcuffed me. The three inmates, who I'd been joking around with earlier in the day, were cuffed also. They marched us through the deserted compound and into the SHU. Threats had to be made by one of the guards because the other girls wouldn't shut their mouths up. Being led in from the rear was the inmate, who'd poured the water on me.

Entering into solitary confinement is similar to those few seconds when a tornado passes directly overhead. The air is sucked right out of your lungs. A weird stench was strong in the receiving room. It made the process of getting assigned to a cell misery. The intake guard made it a point to say, "What happened to you Hood? You just got out last month without a scratch, and now you're back!"

I didn't have any answers for him. His tone let me know what he thought. My current predicament wasn't funny to me. I gave a little smirk and shook my head. It wasn't true that I hadn't received any markings from that first introduction into the SHU. Those eighty-four hours of isolation had stung me. In the middle of my crisis, there wasn't enough energy left in my bones to entertain the man. So I remained relatively quiet while they completed their intake.

Violating the codes of conduct brought swift repercussions if we were unlucky enough to get caught. It was in the prisoner's handbook, which was given out during the initial receiving process. I was probably one out of a select few, who'd actually read it in its entirety. It was puzzling what we'd done collectively to warrant them locking us all down. I knew sooner, rather than later, I'd find out why.

The building had enough room to accommodate maybe one hundred women at a time if needed. It wasn't even halfway full, so all five of us had our own rooms. I could hear the women from my unit already yapping at the inmate, who'd gotten us into trouble in the first place. She'd made herself a handful of enemies in less than one hour. All my privileges were being taken away once again because of foolery. It was absurd that I was written up for an infraction without being able to ask the reason why. I couldn't sleep too good, feeling like an icicle. The second time in the hole was worse than the first. When no one knew me, I didn't receive any kites. Now I was under duress with four inmates, who I was well acquainted with. Every time an orderly came through, they would send notes on her cart to give to me. When I didn't respond to the messages, they would start yelling to get my attention. We were all well separated, hence the need for them to shout out. Even though I was down the hall and on the opposite side, I could still hear them whenever they woke up and decided it was clown time.

The next morning the SHU routine was unchanged. During breakfast, there were a couple of people walking through, to check on our welfare. After showers the air was thick with the smell of wet dog hair. A guard came to the cell and read my disciplinary case before lunch. I was told the violation was because of a reported group fight. Those were some bogus charges. I wasn't worried about it because no one had fought.

When they took us outside for our one-hour rec, they put me in a section alone. The three inmates, who were friends, were allowed to hang out in the same area together. The girl, who was the fifth person in the case, wasn't allowed to come outside with anybody. I was glad that she couldn't. She liked me more than I thought, and that was the reason for her starting the whole mess.

They weren't doing me any favors by letting me out at the same time as the rest of the women. All they wanted to do was harass me. I was being nice about the situation by not blowing my stack. I didn't want to be seen in that type of light. Getting into trouble without doing anything at all was an unacceptable outcome.

On the morning of the third day in the SHU, the four of us were released. They kept the girl who'd dumped the water on me. It was the best thing they could've done for her because the other women wanted payback. I was glad it was over with so quickly, and I could get back out on the prison grounds. It was early enough for me to catch the chow hall before breakfast was over with. I talked on the phone briefly and went to eat some real food. Never was I going to be associated with those other girls anymore because I didn't need a bull's-eye on me. I hadn't done too well with idleness. The next thing I did after getting out of the hole was contemplate where my next job should be.

I was fortunate to get my new work assignment a few days after getting out of the SHU. It was at the Power House, and it was good to be accepted. A vacancy had popped up around the same time that I was out looking for the best situation for me. The job had a small crew and two male officers manning the facilities. Our duties consisted of going into the units to change out the light bulbs, repair plumbing, pipe-fitting, and welding. If individuals were lucky enough to be a part of the five-member team, they made an apprentice automatically.

It was a highly sought-after prison job. Mainly because of the various skills sets taught. I'd never walked around ceiling beams before until working on that job. I'd painted buildings before, but the experience was teaching me several useful trades. The guards were happy when we were able to perform the duties we had been shown. They were encouraging inmates daily to take the learned lessons seriously and go back to school upon release.

I wasn't thinking about going back to college, though I'd already accumulated several credit hours. I'd taken a couple of on-post courses from the University of Louisville in 1988. My school days were over with for good. There were no worries about what my future job status would be. I was only interested in when the hell they were going to mercifully let me out of my waking nightmare.

The rest of the year passed much slower than I would've liked. I fell into a monotonous routine of going to chow, work, and playing softball. It was keeping me out of the path of trouble, even if I was constantly doing the same thing every day. There was a ot going on around the prison grounds because turkey day was fast approaching. The downtime during the holidays was good for having a better quality of food on the menu, but it made everyone feel melancholy. That was always when the mistakes from the past visibly hurt the most for the majority of inmates.

During the midday of the Monday following Thanksgiving 99,' an inmate was brought in as a temporary crewmember. When she came into the Power House, it was as if a model had entered the building. One of the guards banged his knee jumping up to greet the newly, assigned worker. They must've been hiding her. She hadn't been visible on the compound. Her golden olive complexion, long flowing hair, and properly fitted uniform was flawless.

Everyone had to be medically cleared before they were eligible to work, which took weeks. That meant she'd been held somewhere on the grounds for at least the past month. Maybe they'd kept her in the infirmary or the Shu. There were no more empty rooms in the honors dorm, so she'd been placed with the rest of the prison population. Her name was Wanda. She was waiting for the next availability at a federal prison camp. She was too gorgeous to be locked up. They should've kept her hidden away.

The guards had gathered all of the accessible info and told us about Wanda the next day while on break. She was mixed with Italian and Puerto Rican and was out of Miami. Her charge was conspiracy, and they'd only pinned that on her because she didn't roll over on her man. They would've let her go, but she was loyal and had refused to testify against him. She was in the best place possible for being incarcerated. I'd once been in the worst prison ever constructed. That one wasn't bad at all.

For the next several days, I low-key watched as a few of the male guards were flirtatious with her. She knocked down their attempts like a bowling ball. Not every female inmate who's incarcerated openly welcomes the advances from shady, correctional officers. Most can't stand the police. If an inmate did like a staff member, she would have no problem with letting him know it. That's why it never made sense when some of the guards tried to pressure the ones who weren't interested in them.

A couple of the inmates had been overbold with Wanda just like a couple of the officers were. They'd tried repeatedly to gain the romantic interest of the cute, new girl. She told them that she wasn't into women and was getting married after camp. The majority of the inmates respected their outside relationships if they were solidly committed before coming into prison. Even if they did feel some twinges or desires on the inside, not everyone that entered into prison turned gay for the stay. Out of the hundreds of women locked away at FCI Tallahassee, only thirty percent were into having any type of relationship.

I didn't immediately try and talk to her because so many people were fawning over her in the beginning. Their displays of flattery had probably been something she'd dealt with since her teen years. Once the fires had died down, I went about the business of befriending her. After she'd been working with us for a couple of weeks, I sat down next to her one day at lunch. One of the perks of working at the Power House was not having to eat with the rest of the compound. Since we performed what was considered an important job, we walked around with tool belts and always ate first. Sometimes when I went into the kitchen, there was obvious tension when the head officer in charge was on duty. She knew I'd gained a better job and still ate before the mob. I didn't miss being in that cold ass kitchen. Not one single bit.

What I really wanted to know was how the new inmate liked her job so far. All they had her doing was filling out paperwork. She had it easier than the rest of us. When she did walk with us to the units, she only handed out equipment after we'd made our way up the ladder to fix different problems. Figuring since we were in the chow hall, and not secluded, that would be a comfortable spot for her to answer a question. I didn't want her to feel any pressure.

I asked her to come to one of my softball games. She accepted my invite without hesitation, which was automatically a good sign. We hit it off great from that day going forward. After work we hung out together often. My closest buddy liked her a great deal also. Every day when we weren't out doing something together in the evenings, we still saw each other before the late-night lockdown. We'd have long conversations at our desks during work. We only had to leave the building when there was a requested order or an emergency call. There was a little bit of down time each day.

Working for the compound and performing tasks similar to a maintenance man had teachable moments. It was a small sense of worth behind the gates knowing that we were helping out the other women. Every day, we made sure the prison ran smoothly and without a hitch. Each inmate had certain days off from working at the Power House. When I was not on the schedule, I thought about what Wanda must be doing in the office. I couldn't stay focused on myself. For some reason I wasn't thinking about my domestic violence case either.

There was no denying I was smitten, but I hated it. I didn't have time for what my heart wanted. So many questions lingered in my mind about what was delaying the State of Alabama. I was ready to go to trial and they were dragging their feet. All the girls I'd transferred back to America with were already out of prison. When I'd gotten sidetracked a few months earlier, I wound up in segregation. I needed to concentrate on my case, but my emotions were getting in the way. With a Christmas play upcoming on the 17th of Dec, I'd decided to go with my prison family and Wanda. At some point during the festivities, I was going to privately let my feelings be revealed to her. I didn't want to give a misguided impression things were fine between us as they were.

On the night after the awesome play, I didn't have to get my courage up. I just brazenly kissed her by the side of her building, after I'd walked with her down to C unit. She didn't push me away or smack me. Wanda was receptive to my embrace, and I instantly felt like the winner of a grand prize. She had a great personality and on top of it all was her calm demeanor. It's a precarious position for a straight person to be in when they realize they've become enamored with someone of their same gender. I knew it was a lot for her to absorb at one time. There was a serious connection, and it happened without forcing it.

The following day started out regularly, but it didn't stay that way for long. It was the beginning of the weekend, and most of the inmates didn't have to work. We were allowed to sleep in later and deal with fewer headcounts. The only thing I somewhat looked forward to on the weekends was brunch. Wanda was already waiting outside of my unit to walk with us down to the cafeteria. She'd fit right into her position with my play brother and me without having to be asked to join us. She didn't make it difficult to gage her mood. I was glad to see that she hadn't been spooked and was happy under the circumstances. No matter the distractions that may incur behind bars, we were always acutely aware of the fact we still locked up.

After leaving the chow hall, we were stopped by one of the guards. His name was Officer Trenton. He told the other two they should keep going. He only wanted to talk to me. Soon as they walked away, he started peppering me verbally. The guy was super ridiculous. He even asked me, "Hood, how did you pull it off?"

I didn't know how to entertain him. There wasn't supposed to be any acknowledging or admittance of doing something even vaguely against the rules. I couldn't understand why the guy thought I was a new fool. Even though some of the guards tried to act like they were cool with the inmates, they were known to be a bunch of flip-floppers. They probably thought all prisoners were idiots. Sometimes things are inevitable regardless of intellect. Anybody can get themselves into trouble if they fall into the trap.

When Officer Trenton grew frustrated with my evasiveness, he allowed me to go. I was relieved to catch up with my play family. There were no gangs in any prison facility I'd ever been inside of, but the bonds between certain inmates ran deep. They were relieved to know it wasn't a major problem, and I still had a grin on my face. We continued walking and kept on with our day exactly as planned.

The days passed by quickly after Christmas. Plans were being made by the staff for a nighttime Millennium celebration on the compound. Everything surrounding me was the same each day with the now inclusion of Wanda, who helped to make my time go by easier. I was maintaining in the FEDS while staying out of any trouble. Three days before the end of the year, I was called to the office of the guard who was on duty in my unit. He reported some news to me I'd been waiting for. The timing was absolutely awful. I wouldn't've taken on a new relationship if I'd known it was going to be snatched away from me after only a couple of weeks.

Leaning against the bottom railing on the second-floor tier, my feet dangling aimlessly over the edge, I sat in semi-shock. One day I was in Florida and the next I'd landed in downtown Birmingham, Alabama. Their booking process was quick. The attire was an orange jumpsuit, oversized undergarments, wool socks, and cheap shower shoes. I was there to finally contend with my old, pending charge from 1993. It had originated in another city, but there was no questioning their placement procedures.

There'd been a few difficult goodbyes when I left FCI Tallahassee, and that was it. Once again, the Department of Corrections had shown they were in complete control of our physical movements. They could've waited until after the New Year was over to extradite me. They'd taken forever as it was, then I ended up inside of Jefferson County Jail less than forty-eight hours before the next official ball dropped.

The atmosphere was horrible. They had over ninety women in an area which was best suited for half the amount. There wasn't a lot of floor spacing for the females, but quite a bit of milling around was going on. It was more of a modern facility compared to the jail in Riverside, California. The interior cosmetics were setup like MDC LA, but that was the only similarity. There was a strong smell of cleaning fluid. It covered up whatever the jailers were trying to hide. I felt chilled to the bone. Going without air-conditioning in Lard Yao had made me feel as though I could be fine with or without it. Readily accessible, the cold air was taking some getting used to after sweltering in the unrelenting, Asian heat for all those years.

That's why I'd stayed outdoors as much as possible in FCI Tallahassee. Their thermostat was always positioned lower than it should have been. The cold air was obviously one difficult part for me as I adjusted to being back in the U.S. I'd been in the American judicial system over sixteen months and grateful for it. However, I could've lived without the constant goose bumps.

There were only the basic necessities available. We had no access to a microwave and only two telephones were in JEFFCO Jail. The miniature television mounted in the middle of the pod was barely visible. They had six steel tables with four connected chairs in the common area. The windowless cells were four-man rooms. We were packed in tight. There was a steel toilet with a sink built on top of it. The water was neither hot nor cold but a cloudy lukewarm. It had been a long van ride on the highway. For some reason, I couldn't bring myself to lie down. I was in observation mode and not liking the scenery.

With only one working shower stall available, I was mortified. In Asia, there was an uneasiness caused by never being able to take a shower in my sarong without dozens of women always being around.

Miraculously, there'd been no perceived threats during those four years over there while outdoors bathing. That jail was dangerous on a different level. There were baby killers, thieves, prostitutes and some more shifty individuals in a small, confined area. Some Thai inmates, who I'd come in contact with in Lard Yao, had some of those same types of criminal charges, but the fear factor wasn't the same with them. The convicts in Alabama weren't to be taken lightly.

These women were noisy! If one was acting silly and getting laughs, another inmate would try to imitate her only minutes later for the attention. They were the most ghetto bunch of ladies I'd encountered in my life. White and black inmates alike were running neck and neck in the raucous department. The few Hispanic women who were locked up were quiet and huddled together.

That first day most of them were yelling about becoming sealed in because of the upcoming Y2K. The deputies had put out the rumor the computers might fail. All the chatter was about us being put on mandatory lockdown if that event occurred. A couple of ladies were saying it was going to be the end of the world. I didn't want to hear any idiotic talk, but I had no choice in the matter. The inmates, who were the most boisterous about it, were the loudest group in the unit. I knew they were probably scared. Anyone I'd ever been around in the past, who was extra mouthy, normally was a person weak at heart.

A couple of days went by, and we entered the year 2000 without any problems. On the last Sunday of January, the deputies were cool about letting a few football fans stay out later. We watched the Tennessee Titans play in the Super Bowl at the Georgia Dome on a television with a ten-inch screen. We were told not to disturb the other inmates, who were already locked in. So there wasn't any cheering, jeering, or anything of the sort. It was definitely weird with roughly about five of us spread out, sitting on top of separate hard, steel tables.

I was getting along well enough with my bunkmates. They didn't bother me or vice versa. Slowly I was factoring in what my daily routine was going to be. With no book carts or work details, there wasn't much to do all day but eat snacks or play spades. There was only one deck of cards for the cellblock. A handful of the women were daily onlookers. The chow served was cold and inedible. The only jailhouse food I ate was the dinner meal, which the trustees handed out. It was never warm. Commissary items like honey buns and ramen noodle soup made with tepid water carried us only so far in a day. Viewing the television wasn't an option with the constant chatter and banging sounds. I'd sometimes look down from the top tier at a couple of the imbeciles putting on a sideshow. Jail in Alabama was more boring than watching old paint chip away.

A few weeks into my stint at JEFFCO Jail and after my 32nd birthday had passed by unceremoniously, I'd figured out a daily routine. There were random fights, and I kept out of harm's way. My typical day consisted of rising at five in the morning for breakfast. Even though no guards were in our pods, there was to be silence at all mealtimes. Everyone had to pick up a tray whether they ate it or not.

It was a bleak existence with no real activities around to replace the empty blocks of time. They had a rule that we weren't allowed to lay down on our bunks when the doors were open in the daytime. Surveillance cameras only captured the common areas, so they didn't want us in the cells except for getting commissary items out periodically. Certain inmates, who couldn't seem to stay awake all day, would lie underneath the stairwells and sleep. That was the location where all the tattooing took place. It was the only hiding spot until bedtime. They didn't have a cart coming around with any books or magazines. No chapel, incentives, specialized programs, courtyard, exercise equipment, or fresh air. There weren't any functions to go to. For me, the long hours were spent on the top tier, writing letters and contemplating.

Since I'd been back in Alabama, I was being visited frequently by family and friends. The visitations were brief but uplifting. After my loved ones would leave, it was back to the cell block of boredom and despair. There were women coming and going, but my trial was taking forever to come up on the docket. I knew a brighter day would come as long as the jailhouse culture kept away from my personal space. For reasons that I'll never understand, as hard as I was trying to stay away from any bull crap, it somehow found its way directly back to me.

It first started when I was in the chow line one day. I'd been in jail for several months, still waiting to be called out for court. While I was standing in line, one of the inmates elbowed me. Initially, I figured she was horse playing, and it was accidental. When I turned around to see who the culprit was, she looked back and gave me a dirty look. I was so shocked it felt as if a knot was in my stomach. I hadn't been cordial with anyone except for my cellmates. There was a woman in my room named Tracy, who I'd talk to sometimes at night. She slept on my top bunk, and I'd been more so friendlier with her than with anyone else. She'd sit on my bed, and we'd chat until lights out.

The girl that had bumped into me was my cellmate's unwanted admirer. Her name was Bernice. They called her Benny, and her cell was two doors away from ours. I'd heard them talking about her advances toward Tracy. She'd told everybody in the cell that brushing the girl off hadn't stopped the constant aggressive behavior. I didn't say anything to Tracy about the incident, but I knew a serious problem was brewing. I probably wasn't going to be able to stay passive anymore after that lick.

Of all the women that I'd ever done time with over the years, the different groups in that jail were definitely the most raucous. My bunkmate was the only reserved female in the building, and she was worth talking to. She was an attractive young white woman, who appeared genuine, and didn't seem to fit in the jail whatsoever. I was aware of the fact that appearances could sometimes be deceptive.

For over eight years, Tracy said she'd been a victim of spousal abuse. It'd been well documented. She'd even shown me news clippings about the facts in her case. The last they'd fought she had stabbed her now crippled husband several times. It was making her have bad flashbacks. I had an affinity for anyone who'd dealt with domestic violence issues. Her hands would become shaky and tremble when she'd recount some of the fights they'd both been involved in. A vast majority of people will never understand the mindset of a woman struck violently by a man. It wasn't difficult for me to have empathy for her because I knew what it was like. I listened and encouraged her to stay strong. Admittedly though, the hand wrangling was creeping me out.

It was the highlight of my two other cellmates' day when the deputies locked us down for the evening. They would start talking into the toilets or vents the entire three hours before lights out. It was comical the way they alternated sitting on the floor, sponging the water out of the toilet bowl. Tracy and I would listen to the foolery while talking to each other. One female would be on the floor speaking into a hollowed-out crapper. The other girl would stand on top of the sink yelling into the vent at any desperate man that wanted to talk. Neither one had ever met any of those men outside of jail. Whether they were married or not, some of those conversations were downright filthy. Listening to a guy jerkoff from the sounds of an unknown female voice was a typical nightly occurrence happening inside of JEFFCO Jail. I was so glad when it was lights out and quiet time. Another fifteen-hour day of repetitiveness and sheer boredom was over with.

Finally, after three months of waiting, a court appointed attorney came to visit me. There were a couple of quick introductions. Her name was Nancy Smith. The lawyer was a petite woman, who bore an uncanny resemblance to Phyllis Diller. She sat across a desk from me in the jails only conference room. Then she opened her briefcase and took out a couple of official looking documents, laying them on the desktop.

"I've been sent here as your legal defense representative and as an intermediary. These papers are a formal plea bargain. The District Attorney is offering you a sentence to run concurrent with your federal sentencing. You just simply sign this form, stating what happened was voluntary manslaughter."

Peering over at the paperwork, I instantly felt unsettled. I had a throbbing headache at the time, and she hadn't helped it. There was no way I saw myself signing any plea agreement.

"Ms. Smith, self-defense does not equate to manslaughter. I've been preparing for my case a while now, and I want to go to trial."

In response, the lawyer started bringing up reasons to convince me to sign the papers, instead of agreeing with me.

"Miss Hood, you have a major felony on your record since that transpired," she said curtly. "This is a fair deal. You'll get out whenever the FEDS release you from their prison system."

I'd been staring intently at her, but after the caustic reply, I had to avert my eyes towards the wall. I was hurt deeply and wanted to start yelling out loud or speak in Ebonics. Always holding my true feelings inside when I really needed to act a fool had contributed to my ulcerous stomach condition.

A deputy was standing outside the door looking in occasionally thru the window. I didn't want those two seeing the dejection across my face, so the concealment of emotions was in full effect. Getting locked away in Thailand had automatically caused a moral blameworthiness against me, despite the extenuating circumstances. Sadly, they'd labeled me as something I hadn't sought out to obtain. In opposition of me, there was nothing tangible for the prosecutors office to use. Except of course, for my jumping bond in the Asian debacle, I hadn't done anything else in life but defend myself. I'd been attacked twice by my stalker. The first time he'd burned my car to a crisp.

My girlfriend's house keys had been misplaced by one of her two kids during the commotion. Everyone in the house had panicked but me. There was so much loud wailing going on from his children; it led to their confusion. They were stammering and asking me were they going to be burned alive by their own father. I found the keys within minutes and hurriedly got them out. There was an incredible amount of pressure being thrust upon me that night.

The second time I was attacked by the same guy, enough was enough. Now I wanted to be judged by an impartial jury. While I was halfway listening and frequently looking away, I did hear Ms. Smith say a couple of important things. They didn't even want to risk allowing the case to go to court. Their team of lawyers losing a trial to a convicted felon would've been inexcusable. Coverage by the local news media had already taken place years ago surrounding the burned vehicles and domestic violence situation. They didn't wish to contend with any of that now.

I'd worried for years about those kilos of heroin coming back and ruining everything for me all over again. Once I'd taken off and not stayed within the parameters set by my bondsman, the damage done had been major. When the lawyer lady finally finished speaking, she asked me again about signing the plea bargain. I declined and told her to tell them that I wanted to take my case to trial. She acknowledged what I'd said and told me she'd get back with me soon.

The deputy escorted me back to the pod and everybody was on lockdown status. One of the baby killers had tried to commit suicide with a razor blade but wasn't successful. They'd already escorted her to a cell called Suicide Watch1. That was the second time since I'd been in JEFFCO Jail that someone had attempted to harm themselves. Not quite sure as to why their protocol was to have a census count afterwards, since they'd already handled the problem. It was good to be able to lie down on my bunk early though. I was emotionally spent.

It was the smirk that did it. It made my skin crawl to know a pasty towhead was actually trying to intimidate me! Benny appeared to be manlier than me, but I was sure that the pixie cut and neck tattoos were only for show. After leaving the shower area one afternoon, she'd bumped into me intentionally. That time all of her cellmates were walking alongside and giggling. I was being targeted over the wrong assumption. I'd known what she was thinking.

Sometimes during the day when I would sit outside of my top tier cell, swinging my feet over the edge, my cellmate, I liked chatting with, would plop next to me. We'd talk outside of the cell, the same way we did inside. There was nothing to hide, and I saw her as a little sister. It was pathetic that Benny couldn't accept the rejection. Tracy was dealing with a lot. Going from being a wife, mother and hair stylist, to a jailbird in a blink of an eye, could be nothing short of devastating. The other inmates and their problems weren't on her agenda.

I could imagine how she felt. If you're prone to being in volatile situations, eventually you accept them and sometimes they become a part of who you are.

She'd been going thru marital abuse for so long, eventually something was bound to happen. It was the same pattern in my case. My stalker and his ex-spouse had an ongoing, putrid relationship from the beginning that wasn't completely finished. Had the information been given to me from the start, I wouldn't've had a conversation with her ever.

There was no more of me letting a tough girl wannabe like Benny think that any type of bullying behavior would be tolerated. I was already in a worrisome mood wondering about my lawyer and when was she coming back to see me again. It'd been almost two months since my visit with her. She didn't even leave me a phone number or a business card. The summer was coming, and the jail was becoming overcrowded.

Wanda had written to me from Camp Alderson, West Virginia. We'd been keeping in contact thru correspondence. She'd recently been moved from prison, and I was happy for her, but cheerless for myself. I was wearing out from being locked up. Two years had already passed since I'd gotten out of Yard Yao. Collectively, it was well over six years of going thru hell so far without an ending date in sight. I'd intertwined with the wrong people in the past, but now my lesson learned should've been over with.

It was purposeless to make me sit and wait without communicating. No one had anything to say to me about the status of my case. I had a bucket list of feats yet to accomplish, and the prolonged punishment wasn't making sense anymore. Regardless of what they'd thought or didn't think about my Thailand trip, they knew I'd twice had a dangerous encounter with my attacker. I'd first met him face to face in a courtroom. It was for the communications harassment case. He knew then he should've left us alone after the burning of the cars. However, he didn't want to. Not until his family was dead with me alongside of them were his words on tape. That wasn't what God allowed to happen to us.

I'd never been called a bitch on a voice recording in my life, not until my stalker decided to be the first. What I was later told, that was the type of language he'd regularly used when he was drunk or angry. The guy knew nothing about me whatsoever, except that my vehicle was frequently parked underneath his previous carport. I'd never instigated anything with that man. Yet, I was paying for the conflict like I'd been his harasser.

Actually, I'd been afraid of him, because he had seemed unstable. After he'd burned his ex-wife's car, and then mine, I'd figured he would have gone on with his life. He didn't want to stop. Frankly, only the slightest bit of provocation from an inmate was needed to push me over the edge at that point. I was feeling tense from being inside of a place like JEFFCO Jail. Then, the wannabe bully, Benny, was blatantly trying to punk me. I'd held back, letting the first incident slide. There was no pleasure felt by me while engaging that imbecile. Since she wanted to play hardcore, my interest was piqued. I'd had my fill of her threatening antics.

Three days passed before my chance came to address the conflict with my roommate's admirer. I walked into her cell during the day of our next commissary pickup. She'd gone to put her canteen in the locker. One of her cellmates was in there also. When Benny snapped out of the shock of seeing my presence, she angrily asked why I was in her room. There was also something else she'd started to ask. Before she could finish the second question, I had her in a Guillotine choke.

I didn't mean to do it without a conversation, but I'd pounced on her. I was so enraged; it was as if a different person had usurped control over my body. No longer was I masking my anger at the idiotic inmate, who was attempting to intimidate me through fear tactics. She needed to be afraid of the consequences of her own actions.

She was clawing at my upper arms and lower legs as I was closing off her windpipe. Benny's cellmate was in the corner talking bull crap and telling me to let her go. Luckily, she didn't intervene, and I kept applying more pressure. Once Benny started slowing down with the scratching and squirming, I body slammed her to the floor. I slipped but got right back up and left their cell.

While leaving out of the door, as she was writhing on the floor, I told her to stop effing with me. Then I went downstairs and started watching the tiny television. Out in the open space was the safest spot if there was to be any retaliation. I left that female gasping for air, but hurting her badly wasn't my intent. She needed a reason to stop being an agitator, and I'd given it to her. After about thirty minutes, I wasn't concerned with anyone coming for another round. The deputies didn't hear any commotion. For that, I was relieved. Benny was hiding in her cell, possibly still looking like a beefsteak tomato, but I hadn't been left unscathed.

On the toss to the floor, my weight, along with falling on top of her body, had caused me to smash my thumb. It felt like it was fractured and looked even worst. The deep scratches she'd dug into my arms were in searing pain. Once again, someone's actions had caused my reactions to go berserk. I needed an x-ray, a splint, Band-Aids and some antibiotic ointment. Pride, coupled with not wanting to draw any suspicion and risk getting sent to the hole, led me to suffer in silence. I went on with the afternoon without asking the deputies for anything, not even a Tylenol.

All I'd wanted was to finally hear about an upcoming trial date being set. Ms. Smith had returned to visit me nine weeks after our initial meeting. We were once again sitting across from each other. Inner nerves had my mind racing, and for some reason, I noticed she had on a nice fitted suit. Thinking about her attire seemed weird. She'd come back with news for me, but most of what was said went straight over my head.

"Sorry for the delay. I've come back, Kim, to give you another opportunity to sign the plea bargain. The office of the Prosecuting Attorney has given us their proposal. They are obligated to allow you a trial, but it might take place a year from now. I was told they would need ample time in order to prepare their case against you. I've read thru your file. I believe your account of the events. That has nothing to do with the business we have at hand. It is entirely up to you. What's your decision?"

It wasn't easy processing such an important next step quickly with a lawyer staring me straight in the face. Comprehending fully what she'd just uttered, I started thinking of an alternative.

I asked her, "Is it possible to sign an Alford Plea?"

It seemed as if she thought about it for a moment. After a few seconds, she firmly said, "No, Miss Hood. They'll let you go. In order to do so, you will have to accept culpability in the matter."

So, there it was. She basically asserted the prosecutor was willing to play possum. The final offer was for me to admit guilt for something I'd known was within my legal rights to do. They'd allow the case to be over with like magic if I'd sign the plea deal. They'd made me wait in limbo before. The state of Alabama could do anything they wanted, even if someone were innocent. They had first-time offenders not convicted of anything sitting in jail for months on end. Several ladies had been locked up because of outstanding warrants for their arrest. Even DUI cases were thrown in with women who'd committed infanticide. The emotional toll of being in JEFFCO Jail had been evident after a few months. The threat of having to stay for a couple more years was too much to bear.

Being in their jailhouse for a little over six months at that point had been a terrible experience. I'd eaten so many carbs I was starting to fill out my prison garb. Every week someone was walking around coughing, or sneezing, and I was somehow warding off the germs. Why I hadn't caught a cold in all my years of being locked away was a mystery. Every other body part was having some major issues, which wasn't good. I needed to go home and see a real doctor. My intestinal fortitude was intact. However, I didn't want to continue having to be strong every minute of the day. I needed someone to check on my wellbeing in the free world. Prison, along with a medical scare, will have a jarring effect on anybody. Visions of my hometown were flashing.

I'd wanted desperately to be exonerated not excoriated. There was already an ugly conviction on my record for drug trafficking. It was a difficult case from the start for a woman deemed to be a bail jumper. I should've asked my family to retain a lawyer for the manslaughter trial. I'd thought even a novice would've been able to win a case like mine. The court appointed attorney wound up being a major disappointment with her efforts. She wanted the seal shut just like the prosecutor's office did, with as little work put into it as possible.

I'd missed my chance to testify in front of his family. They'd known bits and pieces about the mayhem their relative had been causing but did nothing to stop him. I'd wanted to sincerely express to the courtroom how horrific each ordeal had been. It was especially traumatic to the children. They were making a lot of odd statements and asking tons of questions. Two things stood out. First, they never mentioned their father to their mother privately nor to me. Secondly, they wanted to know if someone was going to come into the yard and burn the new cars. That was their biggest fear.

Now the possibility of speaking my piece on the stand was gone. There was no way in hell I'd willingly stay in jail indefinitely, just to prove my innocence. I'd gone through far too much, and time was steadily ticking away. My sister had recently had her first child. She'd been so ready for me to see the baby. They couldn't wait until I came to Alabama. My mom, brother, sister, and niece drove all the way to Florida for a one hour visit when I'd first arrived at FCI Tallahassee. I missed my family and wanted to get out.

In my heart, I'll always feel that the case would've never been presented to the grand jury for review and indictment had his family members not slandered my name with the detectives. They had verbalized their dislike of the relationship I'd shared with his former wife and children. They'd even gone to my girlfriend's church spreading around gossip. The closed mindedness had caused catastrophic results.

All parties involved directly with the case knew intimate details surrounding the charge. A couple of the policemen, who'd come out to work the constant domestic violence calls back in 93,' said they wouldn't mind being subpoenaed at the time. They had more sympathy for what we were going thru than those detectives who were sitting in their nice offices wasting paper writing legalese. Having cops out there who knew the truth was the only vindication for me while dealing with the aftermath. That's what I would decidedly rest my soul upon knowing. I then took in a few deep breaths to deescalate my heart rate. That was only a job to Ms. Smith, but my reputation was already rocky by happenstance. A second hit could possibly knock me down for good.

The lawyer lady appeared jittery. Being all alone in a room with a female who'd done things, she hadn't heard of before in her career probably made her feel nervous. However, it was possible, maybe one day, she might meet a drug smuggling client being accused of manslaughter after they'd been clocked in the head by a stalker. That was highly unlikely though. The visitation was dragging, and I wasn't going to detain her any longer with my pondering. I'd been looking at her movements and body language. She had been fidgety, shuffling papers around while waiting on my decision. The sand had run out of my internal timer. I gave her a concise answer while asking an extremely important question.

"Ms. Smith, which form do I sign?"

When the deputy escorted me back to the cellblock, I felt numb. I was becoming so used to pain since I'd been incarcerated, there weren't many feelings left to give in to, only acceptance while coming to grips with the sentence imposed by a disconnected judicial system. All they'd wanted was the revenue dollars generated by another victory for the great state of Alabama.

The pod was in the middle of afternoon chow. Benny and her crew were still constantly checking me out whenever we were out of the cells. There hadn't been any more problems between us though. She wasn't attempting to harm me anymore or give me the stink eye. I got in line, grabbed some food and sat at a table. Instead of giving away the smelly turkey sandwich and cold baked beans like I'd been doing, I wolfed down the whole damn tray. I was so hungry and angry, I even ate the mushy banana.

A few weeks later, in the middle of June of 2000, I was on the move again. Although I was glad to be on the highway and headed back to the FEDS, I was edgy. The fast rate of speed in which the guard was driving was reckless. I was the only female inmate inside of the panel van alongside three males. We were all shackled, and the officer driving wasn't taking delicate care with the cargo.

The transport was going horribly wrong. He'd made the vehicle feel like we were gliding on top of the pavement. There was another guard sitting on the passenger's side, but he didn't complain, so neither did I. We'd only been away from JEFFCO Jail a little over an hour before a detour was made. When we started to turn off the highway, and I glanced at the exit marker, I'd known exactly where we were heading. In my youth there were several times I'd visited the dusty, low-slung city of Wetumpka when travelling with the summer league basketball team. The town had no claim to fame other than the place where the guard was dangerously speeding us toward.

I'd been having mild heart palpitations for the past few years every time something rattled my nerves. I couldn't stop the random fluttering, and it would hurt momentarily after it would happen. Driving towards our destination made my chest start to tighten in pain. I'd wanted to eventually ask a doctor when I got out of prison if he thought I may be prone to panic attacks. Maybe there was some type of blockage in an artery. For some reason unbeknownst to me, I'd always done plenty of thinking but not a lot of asking questions while locked up.

As the officer drove past the fence and up to the guard shack of the prison, I could tell he'd done that type of procedure countless times before. He picked up his clipboard and quickly stepped out. It took him less than a minute to vanish thru the main entrance. The building looked like a huge, white barn. There were several industrial fans with the backs protruding out of a couple of windows. I instantly felt thankful for the cool air I'd been feeling since being stateside because those girls were living underneath fans like I did in Thailand. Constant hot air re-circulating was demoralizing and caused frustration.

There were inmates crossing the yard. Each individual was dressed in white prison outfits with Alabama Dept. of Corrections in bold, black letters scrawled across their backs. Looking at those jumpsuits would make for a long-lasting, sickening memory, which I would surely never forget. They were catcalling out to the vehicle, "Get out the van new fish!" I was somewhat nervous. I didn't want to go inside with those convicts, but if I had to, so be it. I'd probably have to fight on day two when placed in the receiving unit. I knew the caliber of women in the facility because most of them had been in the Birmingham jail with me. They were certified fools.

When the guard hopped back into the vehicle and started turning us around to get back onto the road, I let out a huge sigh of relief. After we'd gotten back onto the freeway, the guard finally yelled back to me.

"I dropped off your paperwork, for the body count. You won't have to go into that place, unless you commit another crime, Hood," he chuckled.

When he looked in his rearview mirror at me, I gave him a sly smile, but there was nothing funny. I'd heard outrageous accounts about utter chaos and blatant officer misconduct happening behind the gates of Julia Tutwiler Women's Prison. I silently thanked the Lord I didn't have to step inside of their cursed building.

After we arrived back in Florida, the corrections officer said it had only taken us six hours to arrive at FCI Tallahassee. I told him it had felt more like twelve. I was stiff as a board but grateful to be under the custodial care of the FEDS. Jail in Alabama had been hell. Having access to different choices of food was going to be so much more appreciated. The chow that I'd eaten in Thailand had been far better tasting than the outdated, unsuitable for human consumption, processed meals served to us on a daily basis in the Birmingham facility.

I finally understood why different activities or work requirements were needed while in confinement. Idle time was damaging to the spirit and body for sure. The Fourth of July was coming, and it was a relief knowing I wouldn't be eating slop or honeybuns on that day. Once they'd escorted me back onto the compound, I strutted around the grounds like I'd never left.

Jumping into a different routine wasn't too hard of an adaptation for me. I wasn't working, but I'd stayed constructively busy in other ways. I'd been back in Tallahassee for over three months. One thing I'd started doing was participating in a new two hour a day personal growth class. It hadn't been available until recent months. One of the correctional officers, who'd been on a short vacation, had come back to work with a course he'd bought into at a seminar. The BOP had approved the implementation of the class for those inmates who were interested. Out of all the hundreds of women in FCI Tallahassee, only forty-eight of us had signed up for the program. That was startling to me. Watching the behavioral patterns of some of the women incarcerated, I would've thought the initial participation might've been somewhere north of four hundred. I figured not every federal inmate needed help with their personal development but quite a few truly did.

The Officer Donato was in charge of the class. He told the particular life coach was known worldwide. A course from the teachings of Tony Robbins wasn't something I probably would've been interested in before. Being reared in the South meant you only listened to your parents, teachers, bosses, and the preacher. People who spoke about enlightenment or money on television were regarded as Svengali's.

After a couple of weeks, I was glad I'd enrolled in the class. It was exceeding expectations. The daily quizzes were informative, and I put forth a real effort to grasp the positive lessons being taught. I wanted to implement some of the key principles he was illustrating for usage in the betterment of my own personal choices once I was released from prison. The majority of my life I had always thought of myself as an upstanding, God-fearing woman. That was until I'd gotten the two felonies in the nineties. I was perplexed, while in Thailand, by my contrarian actions. Within a twelve months timeframe, I'd changed the whole direction of where my stress-free life, had been heading.

Since those criminal charges had blown up my world, I didn't want to associate with the wrong people ever again. I'd taken what happened to me as a wakeup call to be mindful of my future decision making. The course had given me another perspective on myself I hadn't received from all of those months I'd spent reading the Bible while in Lard Yao. It was easier for me to understand what the worksheets and videos were attempting to convey to us in a classroom setting. I was taken by the strength in his voice and the stated belief of his convictions. He was a self-made man, who was explaining how to reach our full potential.

In the proper manner, while utilizing the right strategy, he felt that anyone could achieve whatever they wanted. I didn't intend on filling my notebook with dozens of powerful ideas, but it happened. It truly was an interesting program of incalculable value funded by the FEDS. There were real building blocks being given. Thankfully, our class didn't end with anyone having to stand in the pill line at the end of the day. That's what the inmates who attended the anger management classes would do.

By the time late winter had crept in, I was in a state of wonderment all over again. It was surprising to me that I was still in prison at all. The leniency at FCI Tallassee was refreshing compared to every other place I'd been locked away in, but I was past ready to go.

Formalities were the holdup, and I wasn't on the top of any list to get out. The process of releasing prisoners was exacting, but the lack of urgency on their part was disheartening. The only thing I knew for certain was it could be any day in the near future. Every remaining holiday was notated and checked off in my small datebook with a red ink pen. I was going through the motions of spending my last Thanksgiving, Christmas, and New Year's Day held inside of a prison facility. I was determined to never come back and have to repeat the experiences.

When the year of 2001 arrived and started off slowly, I stayed optimistic. Constantly thinking about when the BOP was going to release me was consuming most of my waking thoughts. It had been over seven months since I'd signed the plea agreement, and playing softball every day was getting to be monotonous. My daily personal growth course was going great. It was so informative I would've stayed in class all day if allowed to. We were given one notebook apiece, but I was using mine for both the class and personal business.

I was becoming so enamored with taking notes I'd started making a checklist of the things I wanted to do upon getting out. I didn't want to forget anything I'd been dreaming of. A motto from the course resonated within me. It was the Officer Donato saying to us every Friday before he left, "If you can think about it, then it is possible to actually do it." Even though he was still the police, I appreciated the man. It wasn't just about punching a clock for him or harassing inmates. He was showing incarcerated females the light at the end of the tunnel if we were willing to work our way towards it. He didn't have to spend his work shift encouraging us, but he did.

Two weeks before the class's awarding of the certificate for completion, we were given an assignment. The officer tasked each of us with writing down the most traumatic event we had experienced prior to our imprisonment, if any. Inmates, who felt their traumas may have had a direct impact on their current predicaments, were free to read their essay to the class.

I could have stated the obvious by dissecting my route from a burned vehicle and tender knot on my head to taking an international flight out of the country. I decided to do myself a favor and dig deeper. Years of sitting on the grass underneath a tree in Thailand had given me hours to do nothing but think and read. I knew the incident I'd long suppressed needed to somehow come up and out of my spirit. I used the assignment to do so. The day our papers were due, I decided to share a horrific part of my past with the group.

You see, I'd never told my mother what happened to me at the age of fourteen. It wasn't as difficult talking to the inmates after hearing their stories. I was nervous with the officer listening to every word each prisoner was saying. I was speaking so fast, I hoped they understood the details. The worst thing imaginable happened to me while on a visit at a doctor. Because of excruciatingly painful menstrual cramps, my mother had to seek out help for me. Over the counter pills had given me no relief. I'd been anxious to finally get a medical diagnosis for my ailment. It wasn't normal to literally be bent over in pain and unable to attend school a couple of days out of each month. There was testing done, and my doctor told my mother I had fibroids. I was given a prescription and a follow-up appointment.

Over six months passed before I was taken back to the gynecological doctor. The next appointment I was less apprehensive. I was thinking he was going to only ask me questions about my pain level, since strong medication was being taken. He was concerned with my current state, but he also wanted to give me another pelvic exam. Why, I didn't understand.

The nurse had been in the room initially. She was sent out after a few moments to retrieve something the doctor needed. Immediately after the woman walked out, he took advantage of the situation and sexually assaulted me. I was in the most vulnerable of positions. It was the grossest thing ever, and it hurt. The more I pushed him the harder he pressed against me. His cologne stank like spat out mouthwash. The room was cold, sterile, and smelled of cotton balls. Though the attack was horrific, it was over with quickly. When the nurse came back into the room, he was flushed in the face but acting professional. There was a twinge of anger in my mind against the lady for leaving me alone with him. I was laying there stunned and too frightened to say anything.

My mother didn't detect anything odd about my behavior when we left, and I didn't allow any emotions to be outwardly shown. I was too scared and feeling partially responsible for not doing something else to stop him. I feared my parent's reaction and I didn't know what to say anyways. To make matters worse, I was in the same high-school as his daughter.

She was in one grade level above me, and we spoke in passing. Her popularity was based upon her looks and mine on a myriad of things, the only reason we knew each other. Her boyfriend was athletic and handsome. Every type of girl was coming after him. Something bad happened in their eleventh-grade year. She had created a racial scandal with a dropped note written to him. They had to both be transferred out of my high school the next day. I took no pleasure in her embarrassment. She had never been racist toward me, and most types like her hid their true nature well. She was just another pretty white girl with a scary monster for a father. He had pricked my heart. Two years after his violation against me, he received his just rewards. It didn't make me happy though. I had no feelings towards him at all. During my adulthood, I'd known the incident had given me commitment problems. I was always looking for a miracle worker to take the pain away.

Anytime someone tried to harm me or my loved ones, I wanted to take the air out of my enemy's lungs in retaliation. That rape had been the catalyst for those dangerous emotions, and I wanted it to stop. The day I let those inmates know the truth about my early childhood, I felt better. It was the beginning of letting it all go and moving forward.

One of the first items on my to-do list, when I got out of prison, was immediately visiting with my extended family. Secondly, was getting a license. I had a tricked-out truck still sitting underneath a cover and a tarp, I was told. After all that time, I hoped no one had gotten to it and ruined that for me, too. I would find out soon if my written request had been taken seriously. There were lots of random thoughts while waiting in anticipation of going home. I had butterflies. Something internally was telling me my date to get out was coming soon. It was a gut feeling. Most evenings after chow, inmates could walk out to the track and sit beside the bleachers and meditate. It was something a lot of federal inmates were into, and so was I. It had a calming effect.

I was unsure of what the recidivism rate was for female inmates, but I'd deducted some years back that I wouldn't be a part of its revolving door. They would never see my face again. The third week of March 2001, I was called to the office of the guard in charge of my unit. He gave me a sheet of paper to be used for out-processing. I had one day to complete the form for clearance. I was being released.

My last twenty-four hours as an inmate were some of the best moments I'd felt in a long time. It was filled with administrative protocol and saying goodbye to a few women. I was grinning and not even out of the door yet! Even though FCI Tallahassee was the only place that had thrown me into solitary confinement, I'd encountered a few positive days while in their facility. I was appreciative, for having an opportunity to partake in an excellent class. No other lock up was investing time, and energy into the future wellbeing of inmates.

That final night, my play family had a mini-celebration in the unit for me. They asked a few of the girls we were cool with to come over to the cubicle. Half of the food was from the kitchen. They had more than enough for about seven of us. I hated to leave anyone behind, but I was elated for myself. On the day of my departure, it was almost noon before my name was called. Pat was the only inmate I hugged it out with. A few inmates were wishing me luck or saying goodbye. That was the typical sendoff. Everybody envisioned themselves in that position, one day getting released if they were fortunate enough to make it through prison without an illness or something violent taking the opportunity away. I was walking in a straight line, but it felt as if I were giddy and swaying. After I'd left the unit and stepped into the main building, everything moved quickly.

Immediately upon entering, I was escorted to the discharge station. Another officer behind a glass partition in the control center took the form saying I'd cleared the compound. She in turn gave me all my personal items back. My wallet, credit cards, old license, disabled veterans' identification card, cash, and keys, were all in a bag. I had to sign a form stating nothing was missing. My family had sent in a package of clothes and shoes per my request a few months prior. It was crazy to look at my belongings. I was sent to a room to change out of my khaki prison outfit. My new clothes fit perfectly. Before I walked back out to the officer, for some strange reason, I folded my clothes I'd just taken off and neatly laid them on the bench.

The officer had already completed my paperwork when I went back to her station. She gave me a packet with instructions to follow once I got home. I had thirty days before reporting to my probation officer and one-hundred and twenty days, before I had to be gainfully employed. They also included a form about going to some other places to get help if assistance was needed. A one-way Greyhound bus ticket was already purchased and stuffed in the front of the folder. Afterwards, another officer walked me to an exit door. He opened it up and told me I was free to leave. When I stepped to the other side, he didn't even hesitate when closing the door back. Wow, it was over with like that. It was the 21st of March when I was set loose from the tight grip, of a never-ending prison nightmare.

There were two cabs lined up outside of the fences, and I took one over to the bus station. I had three hours before my scheduled departure. Everything about those first moments after leaving FCI Tallahassee will be emblazoned in my memory bank forever. There is nothing comparable to the feeling of getting out of prison.

I went into a drug store and had a cup of coffee. Browsing around the store felt like an out-of-body experience. I took my time while shopping, which felt surreal. The receipt given to me after I'd purchased a few items was looked upon like it was an award. I was so ecstatic on the inside, surely it was showing on the outside. There was a lengthy wait in the bus terminal, and I didn't mind at all. I was sitting back looking at the different types of people using that mode transportation. There seemed to be a few normal, casually dressed folks, but the majority appeared to be drifters.

The bus trip to Alabama was filled with several stops along the route. After eight or more hours of listening to a roaring engine, mercifully we made it into downtown Birmingham. I then took an hour-long taxi ride to my hometown. I'd wanted to surprise my family members, so I didn't alert anyone to the fact that I was coming home. I slowly took in the scenery, which was all so familiar. The business districts and famous BJCC Arena were shining brightly as we zoomed past them on the interstate.

There were several changes too. A lot of the trees aligning the highway were gone and replaced with homes or businesses scattered about. Once I'd made my way to my mother's residence, the motion detector lights lit up the pathway. It felt funny being outside in the dark all alone. I couldn't wait to see her. After I'd pushed the doorbell, it was an eternity before she came. Immediately, I gathered that she'd looked out of her peephole. That had to be the only reason that she didn't ask who it was. She just wildly swung open the door.

Hugs and kisses were going on once I stepped into the house. My mom was so happy and animated. We only talked for about thirty minutes before she started making phone calls. It didn't take long before a short procession of relatives arrived. It was a beautiful night. They didn't stay too long past midnight because my auntie had plans for a next day dinner party, happening in less than seventeen hours. After everyone left, I bid my mother a goodnight, and I went off to sleep wonderfully.

The next morning, when dew was still on the grass, I went outside early to retrieve the newspaper. It was an indescribable feeling to walk around as freely as I wanted to. The day passed by in a blur. That evening my family had a huge welcome home party. It was a packed house with more food than a buffet restaurant. There was seafood and soul food with surrounding tables full of desserts and drinks. Several of my family members were giving me clothes, shoes and money. It was a good time for me, and I felt a special bond with each of them. It was made even greater by the gifting of a cellphone from one of my favorite cousins. I would've never asked them for everything I was receiving. Their show of love and devotion had me speechless.

For a couple of days afterwards, I relaxed and took it easy. My truck was exactly in the same shape in which it was left. I had purchased it about a month after my vehicle was burned, so it was still relatively new. I'd also gotten a temporary driver's license without having to retest and opened a bank account. Days were moving swiftly. I went out seeking employment after three weeks. My mother wanted me to not be in a rush, but I had plans.

Getting started immediately on making money and not relying on my family was one of them. There were statistics about the difficulties of finding work locally for people who weren't ex-offenders. It was reported that even college graduates were struggling in the workforce. I didn't let it deter me. I'd filled out an application from a temporary agency. I was deemed to be overqualified for the low skilled jobs offered. They still hired me, even with the felonies. I started working the next morning and was off to the races.

So far, every day was moving along without a hitch. I was working twelve-hour shifts. My immediate family was super supportive, and everything was going smoothly. I was living with my mother, and we had no problems. After I'd been out for twenty-eight days, I went downtown to do my initial reporting to the probation officers. Unfortunately for me, I was on sixty months federal probation and thirty-six months with the state. The buildings weren't too far from each other, so I'd decided to stop by both places. After meeting my individual probation officers, I was left puzzled.

One of them was a nice, personable white woman, who seemed confidant in her job. The other one was a mean-spirited black woman, who was skeptical as soon as I'd sat down in her office. I didn't understand why she was so miserable and suspicious. She'd only met me for the first time, a total of thirty minutes. The probation officer's whole attitude stunk, and her energy was way off. I was in complete control of my faculties, but I hated that was the start of my state supervised release. It didn't seem to go well. That was my city, and I was being spoken to like the downtrodden.

Their monitoring methods and procedures were crucial to the evaluation process. I understood completely. When I was released from prison, it didn't mean I was completely free. Screwing up probation was not an option, and I didn't intend on messing it up. I was going to be subjected to two separate officers dropping by for scheduled home visits. There would be random drug tests administered and a monthly restitution payment to make. All the while, I was maintaining and reintegrating myself back into society. It didn't seem insurmountable. However, I could tell that one of my probation officers was going to test the limits of what was decent and acceptable to be discussed.

You think that you've seen the worst of the worst in people already. You want no semblance of a problem in your future. You hope for the best outcome. You recall failure isn't written down anywhere in your journals. You recognize trouble can appear in an instant. You realize there's a confluence of paths to a river. Then something, in the far recesses of your mind, reminds you every demon likes to provoke. It's the one thing they're exceptional at. The response to the provocation is what determines whether you sink or swim.

SEVEN CALENDARS

"Well, I've never heard of a case like yours before," Mrs. Templeton said, looking so baffled her frown lines showed, "This one is intense." I knew her facial expression was only a natural reaction to an outlandish tragedy. That was all gone away from me forevermore. I wondered if I'd be forced into reliving the painful memories from my time spent behind the concrete walls of Lard Yao every month. It was only my second time reporting to the federal probation officer. She was inquisitive. Since she appeared to be somewhat fascinated, and not merely prodding, I answered her as honestly as possible.

I felt a bit uneasy by her line of questioning. I didn't understand her wanting to hear details about the most brutal time in my life. It seemed to me as though my current daily status should've sufficed. She'd asked me about Thailand almost as soon as I'd sat down in her ginormous office. It was a room fit for an army sergeant major, so I was imagining what her past credentials were. The plaques adorning the wall gave a glimpse into her crowning achievements.

After spending an hour appeasing the Feds, it wasn't a long drive over to the other probation officers building. The atmosphere there was the polar opposite. I'd been the only person sitting on a bench upstairs at the downtown federal building. At the state's probation office, the differences were glaring. There was a minimum of about sixty ex-convicts all crammed into a tiny waiting room. On the second visit for my state probation, the time spent mirrored the first one. The probation officer was a visibly unhappy woman.

She imposed a few restrictions and reviewed several rules. The strict conditions of not consuming alcohol or any drugs wasn't a punishment to me. However, the no contact rule amongst felons seemed unrealistic. Interestingly, she took the time to ask me how I would deal with a high-risk crime scenario if the subject was broached in the future. I took a conciliatory tone with my answer. There was no reason for me to make her feel as though I would be a difficult case for her to manage. She could've told me to stand on one leg for an hour each day, and I would've said okay. I was so thankful to be home; I wasn't concerned about any minor hurdles. The freedom to walk into a mall again, whenever I wanted to, was beyond priceless.

When my time was up at the probation office, I drove to work early, the worst job assignment ever created. It was at a raw, metals warehouse out in the boondocks. My residence in Gadsden was a minimum of forty-five minutes away from the site. I absolutely dreaded going into the building. My last job working in the civilian sector had been when I was a sixteen-year-old working for my grandfather. That had been fun. As we tried to get the job done, there were workers constantly stepping away from their duties and loudly complaining every day about any little issue.

It was hard work but doable. There were freshly cut sheets of metal sliding down a conveyor belt. Each one had to be caught by somebody on the line and placed in a bin. They were sharp, heavy pieces. I was getting nicked even with gloves and arm guards on. The people, who became skilled with running the lines, were eventually moved into better positions within the plant. Every job in there appeared to be almost as laborious as the next. There was an enjoyment from being paid weekly, but I hated the work. I was worthy of more than a low-end job and deserved better.

Getting used to it couldn't come soon enough because there was no other choice for me. I'd resorted back to my old days of showing a good work ethic. I wanted the supervisor to visually notice I was worthy of getting off the line before my hands were turned into chopping boards. After spending the majority of the day completing all of the tasks I was given, shift change brought about a welcomed relief.

I wasn't hanging out with old friends or making any new ones. My family was large enough. Whenever I wanted to chill out with someone, I would call one of my relatives. Everything was moving in a comfortable groove. After a few months of being released from prison, I tried blocking out knowledge of all the bad events occurring in other places around the world. The daily newspaper was not always read and the evening news shows mainly reported bad tidings. I had enough on my agenda to worry with and maintain. I didn't really want or need to hear any horrible news stories.

On certain days when I'd catch a health or cooking segment on television, I'd watch it in its entirety. On one of my off days, I awoke to some dreadful news. It had me crying for at least three hours. I'd been home a little over five months after being incarcerated for seven calendar years. During the time in which I was locked up, I'd barely dropped tears twice, and that had been for a few moments. I'd only cried uncontrollably hard after my first real breakup, and when my parents divorced in my teens. Tragic events happening in real time nationally had my world put on pause. I boohooed like a kid until I emptied out a box of Kleenex's.

All over each channel, they were airing live shots of one of the twin towers billowing smoke from its center. It was the 11th of September, and I was watching New York City, in crisis. When a plane hit the second tower, it was all quickly understood. The United States of America was under attack. It was one of the saddest feelings. In my gut, I knew some of those people were burning alive. Then the two buildings crumbled into a pile of flaming rubbish. Dust and debris clouds were pushed into the streets of Manhattan in waves.

It put so much more of my life into perspective. I was fortunate to have another crack at living a life full of integrity without keeping secrets. There was unrelenting sadness for those individuals who'd lost their lives. Their families would forever hold the same disturbing images in their minds as the rest of the Americans witnessing the massacre. There were also reports that the Pentagon had been hit. The nationalities of the terrorist were immediately speculated upon by the media. I'd been transfixed by the unsettling pictures, but it eventually wore me down watching the repeat footage all day. Really, I couldn't wait to embrace my mother when she came home from work. I was grateful to be home from prison and had a chance to do so.

For several months following the terrorist attacks, which were orchestrated by a foreigner named Osama Bin Laden, the local communities started rallying together displaying their patriotism. The stars and stripes were now flying outside of several homes. Americans, who would never make it through the rigors of the military, were proudly wearing camouflage. Even one of my uncles who was as unpatriotic as they come had a mini-flag attached to his car antenna. It was a strong show of support as Americans because our military service members were being dragged into yet another war.

Time was flying by. I'd experienced old holiday traditions with my loved ones and had a newfound appreciation for the sanctity of family meals being shared together. However, my job was still crappy. I'd requested to be placed on another work assignment when one was made available through the temp agency. There was no way I was going to be hired on as an employee at anyone else's company with two felonies on my record. I had to stick it out with the route I was taking for employment.

After my 34th birthday in February 2002, I decided ten months of working in the sheet metal factory was more than enough. My hand had gotten cut one day. It was deep enough to actually cause throbbing pain, which was my stopping point with them. I clocked out and went over to the temp agency to fill out an accident report. They sent me on another job site. There was a position which mysteriously opened. They saw the jeopardy in losing a good worker, who never missed a day of work or was late. There were people being no-shows for work assignments frequently because of illness and laziness. It made the situation better for me.

The truth of the matter was that I couldn't quit working for them even if I'd wanted to. They were the best thing going for me because my options were basically nonexistent. They didn't care who you were or about your pedigree.

One of my younger cousins had started working at the sheet metal plant after he'd seen how easy it was to go through an agency. If I felt he should've stepped away from the plant with me, I definitely would've said something. What happened to him the day after I had left the job was most terrifying.

I received a call from my aunt saying she was on the way to the hospital. My cousin, who I'd encouraged to get a job, in order to pay child support to the mothers of his children, was in the middle of major surgery. At the sheet metal plant, he'd been in a bloody accident. He'd been working at one of the machines, and it jammed on him. Instead of him seeking assistance from his foreman, he attempted to shake loose whatever was stopping the blade. His machine was designed to cut the longer pieces of sheet metal into smaller ones. Something happened, and before he could move out of the way, the mechanism became unstuck, viciously slamming down on his arm. It was sliced at the elbow. She told me it was nearly severed. His life was going to be altered for a long time. I immediately felt a tremendous amount of guilt, and it wasn't because of my cousin's arm.

A few months back, right around Christmastime, I went to a party. It was the first invite for me during the holidays that didn't involve a member of my family. Everything had gone great, and I'd left sometime after midnight. On the way home, I was on a two-lane highway I'd driven on, thousands of times in the past. About halfway to my house, I nearly collided with another truck. He barreled past me like I wasn't moving, but I was doing over seventy. I recognized what was going on.

The moment before impact, I swerved to the right. There was a car in that lane already, and how we didn't crash into each other was divine intervention. My right foot was shaking uncontrollably because he'd scared me so bad. When I looked into my rearview mirror, the car I'd cut off was pulling onto the median. He scared the crap out of them too. I kept on going because I didn't have enough sense to pull over and gather my wits. I should've stopped also.

The next morning my mother was talking to me about an article she read in the paper. It was about a guy in a truck killing two people in a traffic accident, and where it had taken place. I was sickened and shaken to my core. That was the man who'd barely missed me for sure. I was lucky to have dodged him, but I didn't share the information with anyone. I would've told my mom, but she didn't need to worry about her grown daughter any more than she was doing already. Ever since I'd graduated from high school, I would always correlate anything that happened to me in a spiritual sense, whether it was good or bad. My hand being cut the day before his accident was too much of a coincidence for me, especially since my soul was always being tugged on. I didn't feel as though I was doing what was required of me as a Christian. I had a semi-clear mind and was living a celibate life, but I wasn't changing into a saint. After all I'd seen and been through, I'd felt compelled to share with my peers all about my prison dreams and visions. It was what I needed to relieve the gnawing inside of my soul. It wasn't happening though. For certain reasons, I wouldn't speak out. I still had sexually sinful thoughts, and I wasn't a hypocrite. I didn't feel clean enough to talk about godly things. I was clear on what my desires were. They were seriously clashing with my beliefs, so I quietly kept living my life.

Around the summer of 2002, the temp agency pulled a group of its most reliable workers and sent us on a new assignment. It was working at a chicken plant named Keystone Foods. I had no idea what we were about to do. If I'd known the details of what the job was like, I would've declined the offer. We didn't have to go through anything special but a quick orientation. Afterwards, we were outfitted like we were about to camp out in an igloo. A hair net, smock, jacket, gloves, and rubber boots rounded out the attire. I wasn't given any other directions other than what line to report to. After that, everything went downhill fast.

The chicken plant is a wearisome job. They had us under a watchful eye working beside a fast-moving conveyor belt. Dutifully, we were flipping over ice cold freshly seasoned meat. We have to separate and spread them out to cook evenly as we stood in what is tantamount to a deep freezer. It would slowly move the meat into an oven for processing and then come out of the machine on the other side in droves. Everything about working menial jobs was taxing. I had the line supervisor and the other workers laughing at me. I kept talking about how cold it was! I really didn't know if anemia was the culprit, but something was seriously wrong.

The other workers seemed to be managing the temperature, but I couldn't take it. I was allowed to take several breaks, but in the days following, I had to get with the program. Once I was being chosen for overtime hours, and the money was flowing right, I didn't mind the absurd working conditions as much. I was doubling my restitution payments to get the proverbial monkey off my back and taking good care of myself. I was even able to pick up a bill at home to show my mother I appreciated her. She didn't need my assistance, but it was the right thing to do. Being on probation was forcing me to work like a Hebrew slave.

As soon as I started adjusting to working at the chicken plant, the line supervisor hit me with some untimely news. She told me they only kept a few temporary workers and let the slackers go. I had reached the ninety-day limit, but they wanted me to stay on the line. She also told me I would have to fill out an application for permanent employment. When she gave me that dreadful news, the air was sucked right out of my lungs.

I had to tell her the deal with me. I liked her as a boss. The job was tedious, but it wasn't insufferable. However, none of that mattered because I couldn't do what she was asking of me. After I told her I was on probation, she seemed taken aback but not totally shocked. She had a nephew on parole, so her sympathy level was intact. I wouldn't be able to fill out the forms and she agreed. It would be an utter waste of time and an embarrassment. She told me that anyone who failed to pass the background check was released from the plant as far as she knew. I figured that would be the case. She then asked me to continue working until they made it an issue. I was still on the temp's payroll, so that's what I did.

After about five months of me working at Keystone, I was called into a room and told to go speak with the administrative officer. I hesitated but went in. She didn't ask me anything. I was handed a pen and told to fill out some papers. An assessment for permanent hire needed to be made. There consideration was cool, but it was a terrible dilemma. I didn't want them to know the agency had sent over someone unviable.

I asked if I could fill out the papers at home and bring them in when I came back to work. She said it wasn't a problem. With that, I left her office. I felt bad about my misfortune, but there was nothing I could do. According to my coworkers, I looked mopey on the line. They didn't know the half of it. I felt like shit on a stick. When my shift was finally over, one of the craziest things ever suddenly happened right in front of me.

I was driving home but decided to stop at the twenty-four-hour corner store. Everything that'd transpired earlier in the day was still swarming my thoughts. I purchased a few snacks and got some gas. It was fairly late, possibly eleven-thirty at night. When I got back on the highway, there was an eighteen-wheeler driving past me going too fast, but that was typical on that stretch of road. What happened next wasn't.

As he made the bend on a hairpin turn, some of his cargo fell out. It was a poultry truck. At least six birds were dumped out. One car further ahead of me was barely able to maneuver away from hitting them.

Strangely, I slowed and found a safe spot to stop a few meters ahead. I ran back to where the animals were and stepped onto an active highway to save those chickens from being crushed to death. I shooed them into a ditch and ran back to my truck. When I arrived home, and sat in my vehicle for a few minutes, I was spent. I didn't know why I even cared about something so small and unimportant in life, but I did.

The next morning, I couldn't wait to go back down the road where the incident had taken place. I didn't know what I was expecting. They were gone. I was hopeful that they'd instinctually figured out what to do and not gotten themselves caught for someone's dinner plate. On my way back home to eat breakfast, I decided to not go back to work at the processing plant. I didn't think I was supposed to after all that zaniness. I was becoming emotionally soft as butter.

Near the early part of 2003, I was sent to work at a dry cleaner. It was the hottest most boring piece of crap job assignment thus far. I couldn't believe what people had to do in order to survive in the civilian workforce. I would've preferred parachuting out of a helicopter to the grunt work of steam pressing pants and shirts. I'm not the complaining type, but the job was nothing short of ludicrous. The supervisor was hands on. Whenever we completed our tasks, a laundry bin was immediately refilled with hot, chemical smelling clothes. There were a lot of people quitting instead of doing the temp jobs they were sent out on. I wasn't afforded the same opportunity. I had to work whatever was assigned to me and be gracious about it.

On one of my days of getting home late after being a presser all day, I was tired. My mother greeted me in the living room, which was different. I would usually find her in the kitchen or her bedroom. She handed me my mail. I said thanks and went to my room. As I was thumbing through the pieces, one stood out. It was a letter from Wanda. I was nervous as hell. I'm sure my mother had glanced at the postmark and return address. Normally inmates meeting in prison are like two ships passing in the night. They don't expect to see each other again.

I ripped the letter open and read thru it fast. She'd written to let me know her incarceration was nearing the end. She was being released and was going home within the month. Everything had gone well, and her parents were driving to the camp to pick her up. She asked me when my probation was going to be over. There was another question she asked me, which was so damn scary. I dropped the correspondence onto the floor.

In the summer of 2003, I was assigned to a lawn and garden plant in Attalla. I thought the Bayer Corporation only made pharmaceuticals, but I was shown differently. They were in the pesticide business, too. It was a crazy job. I was tasked with stacking pallet after pallet of one- hundred-pound bags filled with soil or fertilizer. The spray bottles were even worst. Some weighed next to nothing while others felt like fifty-pound jugs. They had to be stacked in the shipping boxes properly or the cases would tip over. There were a lot of temporary workers. Someone, who didn't need to work so hard in such heat, would never apply for that type of job. The few permanent workers they had were mainly uneducated. The educated people were in the offices or in supervisory positions.

The work assignment lasted until the winter months, and they let go of all the temporary workers, except eight people per shift. I was the only female chosen in my group. The job had slowed down considerably, but they had enough work for the skeletal crew that was left. I'd learned how to drive a forklift over the past few months and received my license. That was the only reason why they'd kept me on. My work ethic was secondary. Not many people had mastered the skill set of maneuvering a heavy machine around without puncturing the sacks or punching holes in the bottles.

We had an easygoing supervisor, and he was laid back since the building was devoid of the big bosses. There was a daily quota of shipments to be sent out even when it wasn't peak season. We would bust our rumps for six hours straight. Then we'd play card games for money during the last two hours. Even though the job was mentally and physically demanding, I liked it. We were doing what the company wanted and getting paid to goof off, too. It didn't hurt that my supervisor was a black man. I'm sure if it had been a corny guy, the chill time would've never begun.

The three Caucasian men, who were our coworkers, enjoyed the flexible conditions as well. I was concerned about them telling on us, but unbelievably they stayed mum about the situation. Some of the guys, who didn't have money to play with, would stay on their phones until time to clock out. All was well within the plant for months until I ran across a problem. It definitely would've caused the surrounding neighborhood to become contaminated had I not caught the culprit in time. I wish I hadn't been the one to see the crap though. I had to unzip my damn lips and say something.

On a Friday, I'd seen some pallets leaning over in the back of the warehouse. I went into work early the next Monday to straighten them out. In the very back of the building, there were a couple of first shift workers, pouring pesticides out of the back door. Bottles upon bottles were empty and piled high in a trash bin. I didn't even ask why they were doing it. I simply pulled my forklift close. I told them the proper way to dispose of expired liquid materials. They looked at me like I was stupid, but I wasn't playing any games. I backed out and went on with my job.

There were a couple of families I'd known who lived in the area, and deformities from ground pollutants seemed plausible to me. It wasn't my family at risk, but I felt obligated to intervene. Their city water source was nearby. Dumping contaminates in that way was callous. It was against OSHA's rules anyway, so I didn't give a damn who liked what I had to say. The only problem that day were the feelings I had toward myself.

I wish I didn't have worries about anybody other than myself. Most people know how to behave in that manner. Even when something was for the greater good, not minding my own business had proven to be dangerous for me in the past. I still couldn't grasp the concept of *"it's not my problem to contend with."* To me, it seemed weird I couldn't stop it.

In the summer of 2004, I was released two years early from federal probation. The state probation was over with also. I had no problems or incidents during the three years. My restitution was paid in full. My legal commitments were finished. It was the first time in over ten years I could honestly say I was a free woman. I was ecstatic to be able to tell my mother and a few other people about the good news.

I started working even longer hours that summer. There was a certain amount of money I was saving for a move. My mother didn't know about it. When she found out, she didn't like it. I was a thirty-six-year-old, who didn't want to continue staying at home with my mom like a child hiding from responsibilities. I needed my own place. That's what I'd always been accustomed to. I wanted to restart my life and was going to do it quickly.

When the fall blew in, I was ready to relocate. I told my immediate family about three weeks before my departure. Every one of them balked at the idea. They were all worried about me getting into trouble. I was astonished. If there was something I could've said at the time to make them not have reservations, I would've. The only thing that I could do was promise them I'd never get myself jammed up again. I knew it to be true in my heart, but I wanted them to believe it in theirs because I was leaving regardless.

That November Wanda flew into town. She wanted to help me drive down to Florida. We had been keeping in constant contact with each other after she had written a letter stating that she wanted to pick up where we had left off once my probation was over. That startled me; I hadn't completely believed everything we'd talked about over the phone was possible. She was showing me otherwise. I didn't think she wanted a serious relationship with me let alone wanting to move me into her condo. It had been discussed for months and it was going to happen. Before we took off for her city, I told her I wanted to take her to a bed and breakfast in Northern Alabama. It was a detour I'd hoped she would love. I was such a nature lover and hopeless romantic. I couldn't see her not becoming enamored with the beautiful scenery. I was definitely wrong about that. When we arrived in Mentone that night, everything was fine. The next morning, I asked her if she would hike with me to one of my favorite spots, and all hell broke loose.

I assumed it was going to be a normal hike with a newbie. It wasn't though. We started out on a trail that was rocky and she was sliding from the beginning. I was laughing and being encouraging, but she wasn't in the mood. Every few steps she took her feet would slide out from underneath her, and she was bouncing on her knees each time. I was beginning to feel guilty already. The temperature was cool, and the fall colors on the tree leaves were awesome, but Wanda was struggling. The hike to the top of the mountain was a little over four miles long. We weren't walking fast at all. Every so many feet, she would just stop without saying anything and rest. I couldn't understand why the young woman, who barely weighed one hundred pounds, was that tired. We hadn't walked two miles. She even told me her chest was hurting, and her legs were cramping. It was turning into a disaster.

Once we mercifully made it to the top, the view was perfect, but she didn't seem too impressed. I'd pointed down to some people fishing, and she cut her eyes at me like I was a stranger. Maybe I was though. I was passionate about the outdoors and she wasn't. On the way back down, she talked without any attitude. I supposed she was glad to get the hell off the trail. I didn't know what to make of it all, because I never went without my partners on any nature jaunts. After witnessing her behavior, I would have to reconsider that notion.

When we arrived in Florida, it didn't seem at all like what she'd described over the phone. Her condo was in a city called Miami Lakes. Looking at all the Hispanics in the parking lot and around the building, she could've said we were in Cuba, and I would've believed it. She thought I'd love to live with her in Miami Lakes. If the first few hours were the indicators of how life was going to be in the city, it wasn't a good look for me. I didn't want to live in a Caribbean feeling town while on American soil.

For the next few months, we spent time adjusting to each other without any hiccups. She was a hostess at a hotel. Since she was bilingual, one of her relatives had gotten her a good job, even though she was a felon. I, on the other hand wasn't working, but she seemed fine with it. She would leave me a sweet note and money on the bar every day before she went to work. I had my truck, so driving around acclimating to the city wasn't bad with the GPS. I wanted to hop on the highway and head down to Dolphin Stadium, but she didn't want me to go. I felt like I was in Little Havana every time I went to any store. Even their local fast-food restaurants were full of foreigners working. It was weird. They were definitely attractive people, but I felt like the minority. I wondered when the Black people with money would invade the city. It was a beautiful scene. Most nights Wanda liked to party with me and her friends while poolside at the condo. It was somewhat fun. Whether I joined in or not, she kept it moving.

After work, she would sometimes call me to come join her on the hotel rooftop downtown for a late-night dinner or relaxing in the spa. During her time off, she was outgoing when it came to her social life. I couldn't blame her; She had no children. Working twelve hours shifts almost every day, when you're young, isn't hard to do. There were a lot of nights I wouldn't hang out, but I didn't stop her. Nothing is worse than a person who's a buzz kill, and I wanted her happiness. Sometimes, I would wonder why she had to stay out until after two in the morning. She had to be at work at nine and was always rushing. I never questioned her about it.

On the night of our sixth month of cohabitating, I went down to her job to surprise her. I wasn't the predictable person she thought. Every day, she basically knew what I was doing, but I was bored with that. When I arrived at the hotel well after her shift was over, I knew where to find her. Once I spotted her on the roof and witnessed what she was doing, I was effing floored.

A couple of her coworkers were sitting on the couch surrounding her, and everybody was getting high. They had made their own lounge with radio music playing low in the background. Smoke was heavy in the air, and a couple of people were using cocaine. When my girl saw me, she jumped up and brought me over to the couch. She didn't even seem fazed. I told her why I'd come by, and she was happy about it. Her demeanor was playful, but I was appalled. She tried to get me to snort some cocaine. I declined, so she sat on my lap in front of everybody. She stuck her finger in my mouth. Then she rubbed some of the powder on my upper gum, and immediately it felt numb. Her friends started giggling while she was trying to entice the situation. I didn't even berate her. Calmly, I asked for the location of the closest bathroom. I was grinning and playing it off like everything was fine.

I hurriedly got out of there and drove back to the condo. Frantically, I started packing my bags, not even pausing to second guess the situation. I wanted to be out of there before Wanda got home. There were a lot of things that I could deal with. Since drugs had ruined my career by default, I had no tolerance for anybody associated with them. I didn't want to argue about it or work it out. I doubted she would understand anyway. She was knowingly taking a risk by giving in to her proclivities, considering her prior mistakes.

It took less than an hour to pack my few belongings and head back to Alabama. There were no salty tears flowing from the corners of my eyes. I wasn't mad, only a little hurt. Never once did I resort back to my old ways of thinking. I was willing to step aside and out of the way of trouble like never before. I used to stand in the way of danger and knock people over because of pride. Those days were in the past forever. I was now gone from Miami Lakes. I cracked the two front windows to allow the nighttime breeze to flow in. That had been the first city I'd been in with a floral scent in the air similar to Maui. It would be the only thing from their city I'd might miss. Definitely, it wouldn't be the doomed from the start relationship I had wasted time on with that gorgeous junkie.

After that catastrophe in Florida, I moved back into my mother's home in the early 2005 but only for a brief time. I had a cousin who worked for a nursing home in

Birmingham. She also worked in the home health care field and was holding a case for me. My mother didn't want me to move back to the big city where all my problems had begun. I was a different person though. I knew I could handle any situation without succumbing to anger. It was technically in the nearby city of Bessemer, where it had all broken into pieces. I would stay away from that area. I accepted the job offer.

Two months later, I was standing inside of a brightly colored, old fashioned kitchen taking in the aura. The house was clean, and the furnishings were old antique. As I looked around the place and knowing that my client and I were in the home alone, I felt a greater sense of self. After everything I had been through, how far I'd come in such a short amount of time was a small accomplishment.

I had a one-bedroom apartment, a new car, and was working every day except for Sundays. My duties were varied being a therapist. It was a demanding job. My client was seventy-eight and ill with pancreatic cancer. I wasn't professionally skilled to do the work, but I figured it out on the fly. I enjoyed taking care of the old guy, and he seemed appreciative. As usual, when my life was moving along in the direction in which it was meant to be, something had to come along and make it a comedy of errors.

In the spring of 2005, I had a fling with a guy named Jerry. He had hazel eyes and was as yellow as a buttercup. I hadn't been intimate with a man since 1988. It had been a long drought. I hadn't missed it.

However, the fellow had caught my attention with his charm. We'd met at a local park and surprisingly exchanged phone numbers. Over a decade had passed without me having any desire for the male species. I thought there was zero chance for a man to infiltrate my personal space again. The majority of men I'd met felt more like brothers to me, rather than potential lovers. I was definitely not submissive enough to give a man what he biblically deserved. That was a gauge into my current feelings towards guys. I knew why I hadn't brushed him off but I should've.

I wasn't too far removed from my last romantic fiasco. My relations with anyone at that point would be for physical reasons only. My life seemed to flow more freely when I was single. I didn't know fully what his intentions were after talking on the phone for weeks. There wasn't any girly giddiness or soulful connection on my end. I was invited to his place after a month because I wouldn't let him come over to mine. He had a nice, secluded home. We didn't do a whole lot of chitchatting. Everything happened like I'd imagined it would. That was until his roommate pulled into the driveway.

We had barely finished being intimate, and I was still relaxing. When he heard his roommate coming, a circus act began. He was definitely startled. The bed was a mess. He was frantically trying to make it straight. There was a cup of soda on the table, and he bumped into it, knocking it over. It was then I knew the guy was scared. At no point did he ask me to hide or anything, but my mood was totally wrecked. I didn't have anything but a Swiss army knife to protect myself. I asked him if I could go to the bathroom. He quickly showed me. I didn't know what to think about his behavior, since he wasn't speaking.

After I'd washed up and stepped out of his bathroom, a female was standing in the hallway. I'm not sure if she was waiting to see who I was or if it was a coincidence. She didn't say anything, and I walked right past her. I got my keys and walked to my car. Jerry followed me out. He was sweating and nervous. I wasn't too bothered, but I did want to know the problem. When I got behind the wheel, he finally opened his mouth and apologized.

He told me the woman in the house was his ex-girlfriend. They had twin daughters and were living under the same roof for financial reasons. They had an agreement that their dates were not to be brought into the house. He had broken the pact. I was probably not the first woman he had done so with.

I wasn't stressed about it, but we could've made other arrangements. The mother of his children would worry about who was roaming around in her home whenever she was gone. That was unfortunate. A one-time encounter shouldn't have been revealed. That woman had a problematic baby's father dilemma on her hands to contend with. I didn't envy her situation. He'd taken care of what I thought I needed. I was glad no explosive confrontation happened afterwards. My personal life never matched my professional one. A force in the universe wouldn't let me sin and be happy. I wondered if I was supposed to have been a nun.

My spring job assignment with the cancer patient ended abruptly after his son put him into a convalescence home following a knee replacement surgery. I was lucky enough to be placed on another case fairly quickly. The new patient was in his nineties and coherent. He had a problem with walking around his home without falling and needed someone to live with him. I had nothing on my mind but making money, so I was alright with the new work schedule. I would get the weekends off whenever his daughter came in to relieve me on Saturdays. He was impressive at his age. He was still able to read the paper every day with the help of magnifying glasses. He had a military background as an ex-pilot. Upon his retirement, he'd become a youth minister. Knowing that, I felt at peace in his home.

There were church members calling and stopping by to drop off dishes of food for him. He was a widow, and his wife's pictures were hung on the walls in every common room. I really like my new occupation. It wasn't what I thought I'd be doing at thirty-seven. I'd wanted to be close to retiring from the post office by then, but that was ruined by criminal choices. I was living a life of servitude and stashing away a lot of money for my future endeavors. I should've known or felt something was about to happen. Whenever there was no trouble in sight, I didn't have to wait long because it was on the way. One month before Hurricane

Katrina blew in violently, causing major power outages in coastal Alabama, I had an unexpected stormy chaos of my own to roll in.

That July, I fell head over heels for a woman in the midst of a divorce. Her name was Marshall, which was weird, but who knows what her mom was thinking. She'd made the first move, and though I gave her a broad smile, I didn't immediately respond to her overtures. I was nervous the whole while she was talking to me. It was one of those instances when I knew right off the bat that could be the one. The timing could not have been worst. Why we couldn't have met after she was single was puzzling. I'd walked into her work establishment for a quick purchase and walked out with butterflies in my stomach.

Nevertheless, we started a relationship. I had walked into her life at the most inopportune moment. There was no way I could wait on a final decree dissolving their union. That was the absolute first time I had met someone who I had an instant connection with that wasn't initially formed from lust. I genuinely wanted it to be the one relationship I couldn't walk away from. I didn't want to play any games with someone going through such a tumultuous period. We took the relationship slow. There were several lengthy phone calls and quick lunch dates before we spent any time alone to talk.

After a couple of weeks of what was considered courting, I suppose, we finally went out to dinner and a movie. It was as if I'd met my true soul mate. We had a lot in common, which was surprising. I never would've believed someone in her marital position could capture my attention to that degree, especially after the public calamity I'd had in the nineties because of a divorcee and her kids. For reasons unknown, alarm bells didn't go off in my head about her. They should've been ringing loudly.

On our first real date, I didn't divulge any secrets, but on the second one I did. I had the urge to be completely upfront with her about my past before we went any further. I told her I was a two-time felon. Her eyelids opened wide and her pupils appeared dilated. She was shocked to say the least. I had to tell her. People in my position have a difficult decision to make when it comes to being forthright about the horrid choices made in our younger days. She didn't seem like she was frightened of me though. As a matter of fact, her reaction became one of sorrow. I was glad she wasn't scared. It wasn't a subject I wanted to discuss, but it had to be done. I hadn't trusted anyone, other than my mother, implicitly up until that point. I wanted that with someone else also.

We both were working long hours and seeing each other whenever it was possible. A few months into the relationship, I received an emergency text from her. She was in the downtown UAB Medical Center because of a fender bender. She wanted me to come and see her. On the phone, she told me her neck was a little stiff, but nothing else was wrong. That put me at ease on the drive to hospital. When I arrived, I was instantly met by the ugly glare of a scorned soul.

Her soon-to-be ex-husband was standing next to the bed. I didn't know what to think about the situation as she gestured for me to come closer. As I was walking to her, I was using my peripheral vision. He was staring at me the whole way. She didn't acknowledge his presence, and we started talking. I abruptly stopped after a few moments. The man would not take his gaze off me, so I said something foul to him. In a barely audible voice, I also told him to keep his eyes on his wife. I didn't want to be disrespectful in the hospital, but I was somewhat perturbed.

I turned around and walked out. Marshall was calling out to me, but I didn't return. I wasn't falling for the okeydokey. I'd promised my mother she would not have to worry about me again, in regards to foolishness. There was no way I was going to play games in life with anyone else anymore. I'd learned valuable lessons from the class I'd taken on personal growth while in the FEDS. They'd opened my mind to the source of why I had a retaliatory nature. What happened to me as a fourteen-year-old girl had been the root. Because of a correctional officer's class, I knew how to walk away from conflict with confidence.

I couldn't quantitatively measure the effect being incarcerated held in my life. There was at least one positive. Going forward, I knew my future decisions in life would answer any questions about who I truly was all along. Prison hadn't stopped me from being a dreamer, but it had tightened my vision. For some reason, I was extremely calm while leaving the hospital. I was in control of myself, and it felt great.

On the 8th of July in 2006, I checked off the second item on my wish list. I had a lingering abdominal health issue from Lard Yao. I was determined to fulfill most of my promises to myself before I became incapable. Hiking the Canyon lands of Utah had been in my youthful dreams, but I'd never made time for the trip. The Mesa Arch was a destination one of my friends had wanted me to see.

Taking pictures during sunrise while rappelling had been an attraction. However, I had to strike it off. It wasn't a feasible idea anymore. My body couldn't do it, so it was on to the next thing. I went tubing down the Little Cahaba River, in Brierfield, Alabama. There was a water park with a drop-off location near the river. They had a guy load us into the back of his truck and assist us by the riverbank where we slid in.

My cousin and I were the only black people spinning around in the rubber inner tubes. It was going to take several hours in the warm sun before we got to the extraction point. In a tank top and shorts, while floating down the water surrounded by mostly young Caucasians, we had not a care in the world. Nobody bothered us, and we didn't bother them either.

I lost a sandal in one of the few rapids we encountered. Later on, my foot scraped an object in the water midway through the ride. I said something crazy and loud. He laughed like I was trying to be funny.

Our tubes had been roped together, along with a cooler we'd rented. It was such a special day, and I didn't want to ruin it because of a rock in the water. I was already thinking about next year's trip. There were talks of an inaugural Polar Plunge near Mobile Bay. It was third on my list of twelve things I'd intended on doing whenever possible. It would be great to not have to travel into another state for the chilly jump into a lake.

We floated to the takeout area where cliff jumpers were diving off into the river. I had allowed a few hot tears to blissfully flow without restriction for a moment. I felt more freedom from the past than ever before. My relative didn't know what the hell was going on with me. I smiled at him when I blamed my emotions on a painful pinky toe.

OUTRO

Bringing a close into a glimpse of my life, I would like to encourage you with one thought. Be considerate of other people's feelings like you would want towards your own. When it seems as if we're losing our compassion in the world, someone can step out of the shadows to show us how to be more accountable for our behavior and actions. It is easy to feel desperation, instead of hope for a better day. With all of the domestic violence incidents bombarding us from the national media, you would think doomsday could be around the corner. I can truly be a witness to what it feels like to experience growth and compassion after several tragedies. Positive changes made from my heart are a part of my daily life now and can happen for anyone else who fully embraces changing their worrisome emotions.

The reality is there are good people doing great works, which are never talked about or given much attention. With all the constant images of domestic violence being broadcast, someone needs to take a bold stand. The individuals hurting the most have no voice. I've been convinced that worldwide there is evil lurking everywhere. The best we can do to stop the rhetoric and become a collective group is to speak out. There is no place in society for violence against anyone, regardless of the circumstances.

I have never given up wanting to show certain people how easily their minds can be changed from thinking violence or retaliation is an acceptable outcome to their problems. I only needed a reason to speak out. When the bad outweighs the good on the news, it is past time to say something. No one needs to wait until it affects their family because at some point it will. I found my way back from tragedy; it's only right to be a lightning rod to spark a conversation.

In other countries there are groups and advocates fighting the cause without any public funding. In my own country, it seems to be the same thing. There are a few non-profit organizations that run PSA's. Celebrities are starting to speak out, which is admirable. Unfortunately, the victims can't relate to them. They feel hopeless. Whatever it takes to bring about a change, and awareness to the hidden horrors of domestic violence, I am committed to the cause. I know what it feels like to believe there is only one option available when in a dangerous situation.

CPSIA information can be obtained
at www.ICGtesting.com
Printed in the USA
LVHW081951310321
682892LV00037B/1752

9 781647 182670